Get a (Digital) Life
An Internet Reality Check

Jim Carroll
Rick Broadhead

Stoddart

D1286056

Copyright © 2001 by Jim Carroll and Rick Broadhead

All rights reserved. No part of this publication may be reproduced
or transmitted in any form or by any means, electronic or mechanical,
including photocopying, recording, or any information storage
and retrieval system, without permission in writing from the publisher.

Published in 2001 by
Stoddart Publishing Co. Limited
895 Don Mills Road, 400-2 Park Centre, Toronto, Canada M3C 1W3
PMB 128, 4500 Witmer Estates, Niagara Falls, New York 14305-1386

www.stoddartpub.com

To order Stoddart books please contact General Distribution Services
In Canada Tel. (416) 213-1919   Fax (416) 213-1917
Email cservice@genpub.com
In the United States Toll-free tel. 1-800-805-1083   Toll-free fax 1-800-481-6207
Email gdsinc@genpub.com

10 9 8 7 6 5 4 3 2 1

National Library of Canada Cataloguing in Publication Data
Carroll, Jim, 1959-
Get a (digital) life: an Internet reality check
Includes index.
ISBN 0-7737-6158-6
1. Career development. I. Broadhead, Rick II. Title.
HF5381.C288 2001   650.10   C00-932830-0

U.S. Cataloging in Publication Data Available from the Library of Congress

Cover Design: The Bang Design
Text Design: Joseph Gisini/PageWave Graphics Inc.

THE CANADA COUNCIL | LE CONSEIL DES ARTS
FOR THE ARTS | DU CANADA
SINCE 1957 | DEPUIS 1957

*We acknowledge for their financial support of our publishing program
the Canada Council, the Ontario Arts Council, and the Government of Canada
through the Book Publishing Industry Development Program (BPIDP).*

Printed and bound in Canada

Contents

Acknowledgements v

About the Authors. vii

Introduction: Keeping the Faith, Finding Opportunity 1

Part I: Myths and Reality. 9

1 Beyond the Hype 11

2 Ten E-biz Myths Debunked 29

3 Why E-biz Still Matters. 69

Part II: Business Opportunities 85

4 Electronic Transactions 87

5 The Customer-Centred Organization 123

Part III: Career Opportunities and Issues 163

6 Thinking About Where the Jobs Are 165

7 What Makes a Good Knowledge Worker? 183

8 Never Look Back. 199

Appendix: Our Panel of Leaders 203

Index 209

Acknowledgements

THIS BOOK WAS DEVELOPED WITH THE SUPPORT AND ASSISTANCE OF many people. First and foremost, thank you to Marnie Kramarich at Stoddart Publishing for coordinating the development of this project. Special thanks go to Elizabeth d'Anjou for her excellent work on the first draft of the manuscript. We're also extremely grateful to our copy editor, Gillian Watts, for her meticulous work, and to the rest of the group at Stoddart Publishing for their assistance.

Our efforts are supported by many technology and Internet companies. We would like to extend thanks to Mike Quinn and IBM Canada for e-commerce hosting and "infrastructure" support; Mark Tibak at AT&T Data and Internet Services for Web-site hosting; Osama Arafat at Q9 Networks for Web-site hosting; Mark Jeftovic at EasyDNS for DNS services; Anthony Bamford and the gang at Media Planet for fabulous Web design assistance; and Dara Schechter and Tibor Shanto at Dow Jones Interactive for access to the Dow Jones Interactive service that was used for much of the research for this book.

We would also like to acknowledge the many Canadian Internet entrepreneurs who contributed their thoughts and opinions to Chapters 6 and 7. Although their names are too numerous to mention here, they can be found in the Appendix.

Finally, the process of writing a book is always made easier by the unwavering support of our families. Rick would like to thank his parents as well as his sister, Kristin, and her husband, Lionel. Jim would like to thank Christa for her motivation and encouragement through some of the more challenging aspects of this project. And additionally, thanks to Thomas and Willie for teaching the real meaning of life beyond technology. To them, in yet another attempt to get things right, the question is: What's black and white and red all over? An embarrassed zebra.

About the Authors

JIM CARROLL, FCA, is an internationally recognized expert on the "wired world" and the Internet, a popular media authority, a keynote speaker, and a business consultant. He is author of the critically acclaimed book *Surviving the Information Age*, a motivational work that encourages people to cope with the future, as well as co-author of the popular books *Lightbulbs to Yottabits: How to Profit by Understanding the Internet of the Future* and *Selling Online: How to be a Successful E-Commerce Merchant*.

Jim has emerged as one of North America's leading keynote speakers, providing motivating and challenging presentations for tens of thousands of people at annual conferences, meetings, corporate events, and seminars. Jim's views are also much sought after by the media. He has been featured and is quoted regularly and extensively in a wide variety of national print media and television and radio shows. He has conducted more than 2,000 interviews over the last five years on the topics of e-commerce, e-biz, and the Internet.

Jim has written many popular columns, including his widely read "e-biz/Digital Survivor" *Globe and Mail* column, which over the years gained a widespread international following for its perspectives on the impact of technology, the Internet, and e-commerce. He has also hosted several audio programs, including *e-Biz with Jim Carroll*, a national radio show that focuses on the e-biz opportunity, and *dot-commerce with Jim Carroll*, an audio program featured on all worldwide Air Canada flights. He writes for many other publications, with the result that he was named one of 50 International Names to Know by the *Online Journalism Review*, a widely respected international publication that examines the future of journalism in the Internet age.

A Chartered Accountant by background, he has over twelve years of experience in the world's largest public accounting firm. He has a solid business and financial background in all major business, government, and industry sectors. He was recently honoured by the professional body that represents his profession by being named an FCA (Fellow of the Institute of Chartered Accountants), which is a designation given to those who exhibit outstanding performance within their careers.

Through his consulting firm, J. A. Carroll Consulting, Jim has provided professional services for over ten years to many Fortune 500 organizations. He excels at helping senior management map out a truly effective strategy for doing business in the new economy. His specialty is helping organizations gain strategic insight into the implications and opportunities of the wired economy at an executive level, and assisting organizations in articulating and achieving those strategic goals and visions. Recent clients include the Electronic Transaction Association, NCR, KPMG, the U.S. Committee on State Taxation, the Taiwan Semiconductor Manufacturing Company, the World Trade Center Cleveland, the International Lawyers Network, Blue Cross/Blue Shield of Florida, ACCPAC International, Monsanto, Deloitte and Touche, E*Trade, Ameritech, AT&T, Sprint, the American Marketing Association, Excel Switching, Nortel Networks, Ingram Micro, IBM, RE/MAX, the Royal Bank of Canada, the Canadian Institute of Underwriters, Royal LePage, Rogers AT&T, BCE, the Canadian Institute of Mortgage Brokers and Lenders, and countless others.

You can reach Jim by e-mail at jcarroll@jimcarroll.com or via his Web site, www.jimcarroll.com.

RICK BROADHEAD, MBA, is renowned as one of North America's leading e-commerce experts, industry analysts, and professional speakers. He is the co-author of a record-breaking thirty books about the Internet, e-commerce, and e-business, including *Lightbulbs to Yottabits: How to Profit by Understanding the Internet of the Future*. Rick is also the co-author of *Selling Online: How to Become a Successful E-Commerce Merchant*, which has been officially endorsed by Visa and is being used in that organization's national e-commerce training initiatives. *Selling Online* has become an international success story, with sales exceeding 100,000 copies worldwide and translations appearing in German, French, and Russian. In

1994, Rick co-authored the *Canadian Internet Handbook*, the first Canadian Internet book, which became a national #1 bestseller within weeks of its release.

Specializing in helping organizations to capitalize on the latest Internet and e-commerce trends affecting their industries, Rick is a highly sought-after keynote speaker and consultant by industry and trade associations, small businesses, and Fortune 500 firms across North America. His clients have included organizations as diverse as McDonald's, IBM, EMI Music, Manulife Financial, Arthur Andersen, Freightliner Trucks, Rogers AT&T Wireless/AT&T Canada, the Canadian Real Estate Association, Food and Consumer Product Manufacturers of Canada, the Ontario Pharmacists' Association, Canada Post Corporation, the Association of Crafts and Creative Industries, the Canadian Association of Management Consultants, Travelodge Hotels, Microsoft, the Government of the Northwest Territories, the Minnesota Office of Tourism, and Entel, one of the largest telecommunications companies in Chile.

Rick is also an experienced seminar leader in the field of executive development, having assisted executives and managers from hundreds of North American firms with their e-business strategies, including leading companies such as Kraft Foods, Ford Motor Company, Bayer, Sharp Electronics, Royal Doulton, Polaroid, Motorola, Volkswagen, Sears, Xerox, Nestle, AT&T, and Coca-Cola.

As an Internet industry veteran and bestselling Internet author, Rick Broadhead is regularly called on by both print and broadcast media for his analysis and commentary on events in the Internet and e-commerce industry. Over the last six years, he has conducted hundreds of interviews with radio stations, television networks, magazines, daily and community newspapers, and industry publications from across North America.

In 1999, Rick partnered with United Media in New York, one of the largest newspaper syndicates and licensing companies in the United States, to create and launch e-Trivia, a nationally syndicated newspaper feature about the Internet.

Rick holds an MBA in marketing from York University's Schulich School of Business in Toronto, where he was awarded the George A. Edwards Marketing Medal for demonstrated excellence in marketing.

Rick can be reached by e-mail at rickb@rickbroadhead.com or on the World Wide Web at www.rickbroadhead.com.

CONTACTING US

We are always interested in hearing from our readers. We welcome your comments, criticisms, and suggestions, and we will use your feedback to improve future editions of this book. We do try to respond to all e-mail sent to us.

Contacting the Authors Directly

We would love to hear from you! Here is how to contact us on the Internet:

To reach:	*Send e-mail to:*
Both authors simultaneously	authors@handbook.com
Jim Carroll	jcarroll@jimcarroll.com
Rick Broadhead	rickb@rickbroadhead.com

Our World Wide Web Sites

The World Wide Web site for all our books is www.handbook.com. There you will find information about our most recent publications as well as ordering information.

We also invite you to visit our individual Web sites, where you will find information about our consulting and speaking activities and other background information on each of us:

Jim Carroll's Web site:	www.jimcarroll.com
Rick Broadhead's Web site:	www.rickbroadhead.com

Keeping the Faith, Finding Opportunity

> *. . . to carve out a place for yourself in this new and strange land, you must be prepared for some frustration along the way.*
>
> JIM CARROLL AND RICK BROADHEAD, 1994 *CANADIAN INTERNET HANDBOOK*

WHILE SURFING THE WEB ONE DAY, WE CAME ACROSS THIS PAGE:

It was, as you can see, a rather unusual Web page. After all, it implied that the Internet was over — we had reached the end! Perhaps this meant it was time to pack up and move on to something else?

Of course, one quickly realizes that it is a joke, one of many such pages to be found online. There is no final Internet page, and no end to the Internet, as anyone who surfs is well aware. With several billion pages and still counting, the World Wide Web continues its relentless growth, at least in terms of the quantity of information online. But the page above seemed to be an appropriate metaphor for the times. We first came across it at the height of the "dot-com" gloom, in early 2001, when a deep funk had set in over everything related to technology and the Internet.

What a remarkable transformation occurred in a few short months! The world had plummeted from absolute euphoria over the Internet and e-biz into absolute gloom, highlighted by a whirling recession and what may come to be known as the "great dot-com collapse." Suddenly people began to question whether the end of the Internet was near, whether it was all simply a bunch of hype — the "CB radio of the technology age," as some skeptical pundits suggested.

Such talk is, if you think about it, rather quaint. The Internet and e-biz remain very real.

We continue to believe that, over the next five years and beyond, the world of business will be forever transformed by the Internet, as we move from a largely paper-based economy to one that is electronic. Consumers and buyers will be more demanding than ever before. The very nature of organizations will change. And we will continue to see amazing technological developments in everything involving the Internet and e-biz. Far from being over, the voyage has barely begun.

Perhaps that is why you bought this book. Even as skepticism and gloom about the Internet and e-biz swirl around you, you remain convinced that the opportunities are there, *because something big is going on*.

We agree. We believe that something very important *is* going on, and that the Internet and e-biz are going to have a profound effect upon our economy, our lives, and our careers, well into the future. That is why the time is ripe for a reality check.

Given the extremes of the not-too-recent past, people need a practical, well-grounded, realistic overview of the state of the Internet today. We need some balance between the wild and unrealistic enthusiasms of the dot-com era and the doom and gloom that followed it. This is what we have provided in this book, by putting into perspective the many developments that we have already experienced with the Internet and e-biz, and by outlining the many that are still to come.

WHO SHOULD READ THIS BOOK?

If you care about the Internet and e-biz, and believe that they still offer plenty of future opportunity, this book is for you. It is aimed at several different groups of people.

First and foremost, this book is for business executives looking for insight on how the Internet will affect the business world — not hype, not warmed-over post-dot-com hysteria, but realistic, practical guidance on how the Internet will affect business in the years to come.

This book will also be useful to people looking for new career opportunities in the Internet age. It's not for someone looking for ideas on how to become an instant dot-com millionaire, or trying to figure out how to make a quick buck. It's for someone who wants a realistic, practical perspective on opportunities that may evolve in the years to come, or insight into how their jobs and the companies they work for might be affected.

The book will be useful to anyone who is interested in important business and technological trends. We think that the reality check offered here will be useful in countering some of the ridiculous and often bizarre hype about the Internet and technology that has proliferated during the past several years.

Finally, this book will be useful for anyone who wants more than a six-month perspective on the Internet. As we explain throughout, we believe that many aspects of the Internet and e-biz will only come about in the longer term. The guidance and views in this book reflect that belief.

WHO ARE WE TO MAKE PREDICTIONS?

In the past, we have guided Canadians through many Internet issues. Our many and loyal fans date from early in 1994, when our original *Canadian Internet Handbook* became a national bestseller. Since that time, we've sold some 750,000 books to Canadians, which must be the best testimonial that we have been doing something right. Perhaps what is most important is that, throughout the early period of Internet hype and the subsequent dot-com excesses, we can proudly say that we maintained our composure and provided cautious and careful guidance that in many cases turned out to be absolutely right.

Consider our track record, starting with the idea of online shopping. While the orgy of enthusiasm for selling online reached a crescendo from 1996 until 2000, we were expressing cautious skepticism as to the eventual size of the market. We were writing a book about the topic at the same time, but we didn't believe the excessive hype, even though we were busy advising people about e-biz strategies. We were concerned about the ridiculous proclamations we were seeing about the growth potential of online shopping, and questioned some of the fundamental assumptions that were being made.

Our thoughts were quoted in a news article: "I think it's a lot of wishful thinking. If I'm going to buy a new suit, I'm going to want to step in front of a mirror and try it on. Just because the technology can do it doesn't mean it's going to happen." In our book *Selling Online: How to Be a Successful E-biz Merchant*, we expressed our skepticism right up front, in Chapter 1:

What is the biggest problem on the Internet today?

Inexperienced people with over-inflated expectations who create online stores, with the belief that once they've done the work, the dollars will roll in. We'd like to suggest that the most important thing you can do in your venture into the world of selling online is to have one, hard, serious look at your likelihood for success online.

The fact is, you might not succeed. You might create an online store, only to find that no one is aware of it. You might fail to sell anything online. You might be trying to sell a product that no one has an interest in purchasing. You might be destroyed by competition that is far more Internet savvy, and that has far deeper pockets than you. You might not be able to keep your inventory up-to-date, or you might have problems in filling the orders you do receive. The fact is, your online store might come nowhere close to meeting your expectations — with disastrous results.

The fact is, you might fail.

While we encouraged people to consider the opportunities of the online shopping environment, we suggested that they be realistic in their expectations. And boy, were we right — online shopping has proven to be not a huge opportunity, but only a minor one.

That isn't the only area where we feel vindicated in our predictions. In *Lightbulbs to Yottabits: How to Profit by Understanding the Internet of the Future*, which was released in the fall of 1999, we expressed concern about overvalued Internet stocks. We believed that things had gone to such a ridiculous extreme that the entire house of cards could be pushed over the edge, causing a global recession, by something as minor as a missed earnings report from Microsoft.

We had predicted fairly accurately the situation that began to emerge six months later:

Our reasoning goes like this: all we need is one missed earnings estimate by a major company like Microsoft to shatter investor confidence in hi-tech stocks. A routing of stocks would have a dramatic impact on Internet stocks. Given the lack of business fundamentals for many Internet stocks, a widespread crash of Internet stocks will occur. That will further shatter confidence in hi-tech stocks overall, many of which will be unfairly punished by the media circus set to ensue. As hi-tech stocks drop, overall confidence in the market will be subject to extreme stress. The rest of the market will begin to drop . . .
Are we overly pessimistic? We think not.

We were almost bang on — it was a problem with Microsoft that started the round of dot-com collapses in 2000 and the subsequent tech-based recession. In March 2000 a U.S. judge ruled that Microsoft was a monopoly. The result was that its stock price plunged, sending tech stocks into a spin, which caused the collapse of many dot-com and tech companies — and so the great shakeout began.

Our track record goes all the way back to 1994. At that time, in our first *Canadian Internet Handbook*, we bemoaned the fact that telecommunications companies had become almost giddy about what they called the "information superhighway." It was evident that they believed television would be the centre of the information-based universe of the future. We were convinced that it wasn't TV but the computer that would be at the forefront of the revolution, and that this thing called the Internet would be at the centre of it all. Well, we couldn't have been more right with that one.

So, if we believe we can do a pretty good job of helping you understand where the Internet and e-biz are going, it's because we've done a pretty good job so far of calling things right.

HOW THIS BOOK IS ORGANIZED

The first section, **Myths and Reality**, takes a look at what we've been through with the Internet and e-biz so far, and where we are today.

In Chapter 1, **Beyond the Hype**, we'll do an intensive reality check on the Internet and e-biz. A lot of water has gone under the bridge with respect to people's and companies' experiences with the Internet, both positive and negative. We'll put some of the issues into perspective in order to give you a good sense of how the rest of our voyage will unfold. We will also tell you some fascinating stories about the Internet and what is being said in the media.

If you are trying to assess your future opportunities with the Internet and e-biz, you will need a clear understanding that some of the things you believed are simply not true. That's why, in Chapter 2, we spend some time on **Ten E-biz Myths Debunked**. The recent excessive hype surrounding the Internet and e-biz has caused many people to develop false ideas of what it takes to make e-biz work. This chapter will help you become firmly grounded in terms of understanding the complexity of the Internet and e-biz, and will help you put into perspective what is real and what is not.

The next chapter addresses the concept, **Why E-biz Still Matters**. Why indeed? Amid all the dot-com gloom of 2001, you may question whether any career and job opportunities are still unfolding here. Read this chapter, and you'll come away convinced that the answer is yes.

Then we'll launch you into the second section, **Business Opportunities**, and take a look at two areas where we think the biggest efforts will be concentrated in the years to come.

First, in the next 20 years, massive spending with respect to the Internet and e-biz will occur as companies begin a slow, steady migration from a paper-based economy to one that is "wired." That's what we examine in Chapter 4, **Electronic Transactions**, where we take a look at the many corporate projects that will result when companies learn to take real advantage of the connectivity of the Internet. We've been saying for years that real e-biz isn't about making money; it's about saving money, and this chapter will outline why.

The next issue that we examine is rooted in how the Internet changes the way in which customers deal with organizations. Anyone who has surfed the Internet realizes that it puts a great deal of power into the buyers' hands. Will this fact lead to new career and e-biz opportunities? We think so — and we outline why in Chapter 5, **The Customer-Centred Organization**. It is an exploration of the many ways in which organizations are going to have to become more responsive and focused on their customers. It will also give you a sense of some large-scale projects and new technologies that are coming up in this area.

Once you have a practical, realistic overview of how major projects involving the Internet and e-biz will unfold, we'll give you an idea of the many different areas of opportunity that will follow — in our third section, **Career Opportunities and Issues**. That's what we look at in Chapter 6, **Thinking About Where the Jobs Are**, an overview in which you can discover unique career or job opportunities for yourself.

In Chapter 7, **What Makes a Good Knowledge Worker?**, we will enhance our advice with some thoughts on key career skills and attributes that will help ensure your success. We interviewed some of Canada's e-biz and technology leaders — some of them successful, and some of them not — in order to get their opinions on what it takes to succeed in the wired economy. We think you will find their ideas and guidance invaluable.

We'll wrap up with Chapter 8, **Never Look Back**. Given the periods of dot-com excess and dot-com gloom that characterized the first few years of the Internet, it's easy to become discouraged when it comes to career opportunities in this new area of business. Some down-and-dirty motivation is required to get ahead — and we're ready to provide it, because we believe the opportunities are huge.

And so the closing chapter — and, we hope, the entire book — will give you the motivation to move forward and figure out where you can find opportunity in this magical world of the Internet and e-biz.

Part I

Myths
and Reality

Chapter 1

Beyond the Hype

The believers, meanwhile, have been getting rich — and seeking justification for their continuing faith. They say the world has fundamentally changed, that we have entered an era of technology-driven prosperity to which the stock market gains of the late 1990s are simply a prelude.

"THE DOW MIRACLE IN NEW YORK," *NATIONAL POST*, FEBRUARY 10, 1999

Can e-commerce bounce back or are the glory days of the Internet over forever?

"DOT-COM BUSTS ASIDE, THE WEB WORKS," *NEWSDAY*, DECEMBER 28, 2000

THE PAST FEW YEARS OF MEDIA HYPE ABOUT THE INTERNET HAVE BEEN astounding. The Internet burst into the public consciousness as no other technology ever has before, nor likely ever will again. As it began to invade our business and personal lives, a period of insanity seemed to take over the world. Think about how quickly things have evolved over the past several years, and of the extremes that we have gone through.

Only six or seven years ago, few people had even heard of the Internet. E-mail was but a concept to most, and the World Wide Web existed only in nascent form. The hot Internet topic at the time? Most people were trying to understand how the Internet worked and to figure out how they could get online. Shortly afterwards came a period of widespread excess, with wild predictions about the future, questionable business models, soaring stock market valuations, and lots of general Internet hype. "The Internet is revolutionary! It's going to change the world! Everyone must participate!" — so went the rallying cries.

Media reporting and Internet hype have been like a pendulum, swinging one way and then the other. The pendulum soared higher and higher as each breathtaking claim was added to the list. And the claims that filled the air were indeed grandiose. It was said that every business had to become an e-biz, or they would all suffer a quick and painful death. Dot-com millionaires were the heroes of the day, and greedy dreams of wealth seemed to take over the Internet.

SOME QUOTES FROM THE RECENT PAST ABOUT THE INTERNET NOW LOOK RATHER SILLY:

- "We have the ability to make every commodity-selling brick-and-mortar store obsolete." Joseph Park, CEO of online convenience-store delivery service Kozmo.com, quoted in *InformationWeek*, November 8, 1999

- "Being a land-based brand is becoming a handicap." Toby Lenk, CEO of now-defunct online toy retailer eToys.com, quoted in the *Austin American-Statesman*, February 27, 1999

- "If you can't react quickly, you'll become extinct." Gary B. Moore, senior vice-president at Electronic Data Systems, on the Internet's threat to traditional businesses, quoted in the *Dallas Morning News*, June 27, 1999

- "Shops will not disappear, but I wouldn't want to be invested too heavily in real estate in the next two years." Nicholas Negroponte, director of MIT Media Lab, quoted in the London *Sunday Times*, December 19, 1999

- "We're going to be unprofitable for a long time. And that's our strategy." Jeff Bezos, founder and CEO of Amazon.com, quoted in *Inc.* magazine, September 1997

- "You, too, can be an Internet millionaire." "Dot-com Millionaire 2.0," *Canadian Business*, February 7, 2000

Throughout this period, we saw the emergence of the "Internet estimate." Companies, consultants, start-ups, the media — all were suddenly and massively hungry for statistics that involved the Internet. Organizations such as Forrester Research, International Data Corporation (IDC), and the Gartner Group found themselves cast into the limelight. Statistic after statistic gushed forth, each one suggesting that e-biz opportunities were even bigger than they had been the day before.

Consider the estimates involving B2B, or business-to-business e-commerce opportunities. Forrester started out with an estimate that it would be worth some $3 billion by 2003. Then Gartner trumped them with a forecast that it would grow to $7.3 *trillion* by 2004. Not to be outdone, within days the Bank of America issued a report that the market would be some $13 trillion.

JUDGING THE REALITY OF NUMBERS

Here's how to assess estimates in a report about the Internet or e-commerce:

• Check the reliability and credibility of the source. Does the organization have a good track record?

• Judge everything by its merits. Something that seems too good to be true probably is.

• Judge everything by how extreme it is. If the prediction looks too radical, it probably is.

• Take time to assess the methodology used in the study.

• Seek alternatives. Look at several sources; don't rely on only one.

• Find out who is behind the numbers. A study sponsored by a company with a vested interest in the results could be less credible than a truly independent study.

• Examine the issue over a period of time. There will probably be several studies related to the topic at hand. How do the numbers vary?

The hype came to an abrupt end with the dot-com collapse of March 2000 and the period of gloom that quickly followed. *Wham!* The pendulum had swung the other way, with dramatic force. Market valuations collapsed, dot-com start-ups disappeared, layoffs ensued in the "new economy," and the tech party of the previous decade seemed to be over. Prognosticators and the media began to suggest that the era of the Internet and e-biz was at an end. Web sites such as dotcomgraveyard.com and DotComFailures (www.dotcomfailures.com) were established, providing people with a minute-by-minute account of the ongoing death spiral.

Next ensued what appeared to be a media backlash against the Internet. "It's all been overstated!" came the cry. The news stories made an abrupt about-face turn:

• *"Dot-com Deaths Accelerate as Money Dries Up: Shake-out greatest among consumer Web sites"*
  FINANCIAL POST, DECEMBER 12, 2000

• *"Much-Hyped E-commerce a Bust So Far: Statistics Canada report finds online sales account for just 0.2% of business"*
  THOMAS WATSON, *NATIONAL POST*, NOVEMBER 8, 2000

- *"Is E-commerce Dead?"*
  BUSINESS STANDARD [ONLINE], WWW.BUSINESS-STANDARD.COM, FEBRUARY 2, 2001
- *"E-commerce Is Dead"*
  ABIX — AUSTRALASIAN BUSINESS INTELLIGENCE (WWW.ABIX.COM.AU), JULY 2, 2000

From our observations of the past several years, it seems that the media and other commentators on the Internet and e-biz can see no middle ground. But remember that the hype that surrounds these topics — and the media reports and resulting attitudes of people towards them — is like a pendulum that swings towards excess, in one direction or the other. The reality is usually somewhere firmly in the middle, as we will see in the rest of this chapter.

In order to make the most of the unfolding opportunities of the Internet and e-biz, you need to cut through the hype. You need a reality check. That's what we hope to provide in this book: a very careful, very realistic, and very cautious perspective on our future.

WHAT'S ALL THE FUSS ABOUT?

Amid all the hype about the vast impact of the Internet, plenty of people still feel skeptical. After all, in many cases both the Internet and e-commerce have failed to prove themselves. Often the hype hasn't matched the day-to-day reality that people see around them, with the natural result that some now disbelieve any predictions.

Consider this example: Around the time that we were beginning our research for this book, we spoke to an association of marina operators. These are folks who manage small- to large-scale marinas on lakes in Canada, many of which could be characterized as "mom-and-pop" operations. Some of their income is derived from renting or leasing marina slips to boat owners and from the winter storage of boats, but most of their profit comes from the sale of boats, boating equipment, and supplies.

During the question-and-answer session that followed our talk, one marina operator stood up and told us that he was quite experienced with the Internet. He knew that there were plenty of threats to his business on the horizon — particularly when it comes to product sales — because of e-commerce. He knew that several large-scale, well-funded Web initiatives focus on the sale of boats and boating products. He could rattle off a list of Web-based potential competitors at the drop of a hat. For example, big e-biz sites that allow people to buy and sell boats online and bypass folks like him, such as boats.com (www.boats.com), were a threat to his own boat resale business. He had spent a great deal of time studying the boats.com site, which is quite sophisticated and extensive, and was well aware that, according to the Internet buzz, it could endanger his livelihood.

According to his understanding of e-commerce, the marina operator said, he should also feel adverse effects from the many online boating supply sites, such as the Canadian Binnacle site (www.binnacle.com). It is only one of many Web sites that feature a wealth of boating supply products, from bilge pumps to outboard motors to lifejackets, for sale directly to boating enthusiasts. In short, he had found plenty of companies eager to displace his business.

Not only that, he went on, but in the new world of e-commerce, his own suppliers might in theory decide to compete directly against him. Everyone was talking about "disintermediation," so he was aware that manufacturers of boating supplies and boats might choose to sell directly to the user. That could have a big impact on him.

The marina operator had studied all of this and concluded that the inevitable result would be increased price-cutting driven by widespread Internet-based competition — a new, far more competitive and cutthroat boating market, one that could significantly hurt his margins.

In other words, he had plenty of reasons to be worried.

But then he told us that, in spite of such threats, he had seen barely any impact. This led him to ask, why wasn't he being hurt? Since he couldn't see any real impact from the Internet, he wondered if he should even bother worrying about it. After all, his customers kept coming back, his business was healthy, and he didn't see many of his clients buying and selling boats, equipment, or supplies online.

He had his own ideas about what was happening, and proceeded to answer his question himself. When someone is buying a boat, he said, they are often looking for expert advice and guidance. A boat isn't a simple "commodity" type of purchase. It is a product that is often highly customized, with various add-ons and ancillary devices, leading to a rather intensive sales process that requires the services of an expert like himself. His experience was that people who are buying a boat often want guidance; they aren't quite ready to do it all on their own. People don't seem to want to abandon the expert or a person they can trust, in order to save a few dollars through a Web site. Given this situation, why was everyone telling him to get on board the e-biz and Internet trains?

Many people who have investigated e-biz and the Internet over the past several years have come to similar conclusions. Every day in the newspaper we are told by yet another political or business leader that e-commerce is going to be big, and that we had better get involved. We regularly read surveys, often sponsored by high-tech or consulting companies, suggesting that Canadian businesses continue to lag when it comes to e-commerce. We are informed that we need to become "knowledge workers," but we wonder if the people who are advising us have a clue what a knowledge worker is.

Many of us have worked intensely with the Internet — after all, it isn't that we're not trying. Over the past several years we've invested in setting up Web sites, have become conversant with the technology, and have dedicated much effort to the world of the Internet and e-biz. We feel browbeaten by the relentless thumping of the Internet and e-commerce hype machines.

Yet, like the marina operator, many of us are perhaps finding that the Internet is having very little effect on our businesses.

The experiences that many people have had certainly don't match up with the rhetoric — the drumbeat of Internet hype — that surrounds the topic. So, like the marina operator, many people end up asking, "What's all the fuss about? Why all this talk, when so little seems to have changed in real terms?"

THE REALITY BEHIND THE HYPE

That's a very good question, and our answer is in three parts. First, in some areas, the media frenzy over the potential of the Internet was, quite simply, hugely overblown. Very few sectors have been completely unaffected by e-commerce, but in many its impact has been small. There was never any real reason, beyond journalistic hysteria, for it to be otherwise. Second, in other areas, the Internet has already had a major impact. People looking for massive changes there are simply looking in the wrong place. Third, in some cases, the massive upheavals are real enough — but they are still in the future. Media hype has led us to expect overnight changes, but many of the important effects of the Internet revolution will, we believe, come about slowly, in the long term.

Let's look at each of these points in a little more detail.

Overblown Expectations

In any number of industries, a comparison of the hype with the reality of what has transpired shows how unrealistic some expectations have been. Consider the buzz that surrounded the world of retail over the past several years. Retailers were advised to get on board the Internet train, or risk being steamrollered by e-commerce. Shrill messages proclaimed that shopping malls were doomed and that established retailers would find themselves in trouble. Not only that, a process of "disintermediation" was predicted, in which manufacturers and suppliers would begin selling directly to the consumer, bypassing the retail sector and causing it great harm.

The result was that many retailers, both large and small, bravely took the e-biz plunge, investing heavily in creating sophisticated online shopping sites — only to discover, to their horror, that few consumers were prepared to buy online. The resulting carnage was ugly, as one dot-com retailer after another shut down. Established retail companies also realized that their online sales were less than exciting. With this failure came a shift in predictions about the eventual size of the online shopping market. The pundits finally seemed to realize that online shopping might never amount to more than a small fraction of regular retail sales.

Once everyone had calmed down, a more rational and careful assessment of the future of Internet retail began. It would only ever be a niche activity, one day totalling perhaps some 5 to 10 percent of global retail sales. Dig deeper into Internet retail today, and you'll find some fascinating numbers that belie the early promise of online shopping. Take online grocery sales: Far from being a threat to established chains, they are now expected to have a market share of $7.5 billion (U.S.) by 2003. That's pretty big business, but it represents only a paltry one percent of all grocery sales.

Or consider the insurance industry. There was lots of speculation that consumers were going to flock to the Internet to research their insurance options and then arrange for a policy online. Insurance products seemed to be a natural for the Internet, especially to insurance companies. Online sales presented a promising opportunity for them to sell directly to consumers and businesses, thereby bypassing the traditional insurance agent. This convenience offered insurance companies the potential for big cost savings.

Forbes magazine noted, "The impetus for more streamlining is striking. According to First Boston, adding a new customer through an independent agent consumes 30% of premium dollars; through a captive agent, the cost is 20% to 25%. Marketing through a toll-free number or the Net costs only 10% to 12%" ("$800 Billion at Risk," November 29,

1999). In other words, they could bypass the broker and sell directly, saving bags of money!

Well, that certainly didn't happen — few online insurance sales materialized in the early years of the Internet. While some financial services such as online banking and investing took off, many others, including insurance, did not. A recent Statistics Canada survey indicated that in 1999 less than 0.1 percent of revenue in the financial services sector, which includes insurance, came from the Web.

The result? Now that the bloom is off the rose, the predictions being made for online insurance sales aren't quite so exciting. For example, suppose that, by 2003, online insurance transactions achieve the estimated $4 billion that some experts are now suggesting. That might seem like a large number, but it isn't — it represents only 2 percent of the overall insurance market. That means that 98 cents of every dollar is still going to be spent through traditional channels such as insurance brokers and agents.

Does that mean that the insurance sector will be unaffected by e-biz? Not at all — later in this book we will put into perspective some of the ways in which the industry is being changed. It is just that the early excitement and some predictions about change in the insurance industry did not come to fruition.

The list of examples could go on and on. Online mortgages? Predictions were that many people would flock to mortgage-comparison Web sites to obtain quotes on mortgage rates and then apply for a mortgage online. But that didn't happen. The most recent estimates suggest that less than 0.3 percent of all mortgages are underwritten online, which means that they are barely making a dent in the industry. Auto sales? Car dealers were supposed to be doomed. Today they seem to be humming along quite nicely, thank you, since few people care to purchase cars online.

Massive Impact in Some Sectors

While the Internet and e-commerce may not have affected some areas of the business world so far, they have had a significant impact on other industries. This raises an interesting point — although the effects of the Internet have been slow to reveal themselves in some sectors, in others they have appeared at an amazing rate.

Consider stock trading, one industry that has been steamrollered by the Internet and e-biz. It is expected that, by the end of 2001, some one million Canadians will have an online stock trading account, and at least one in every four Canadian investors will manage their investments online. That represents a significant change, because the typical online stock commission is $30 or $40, compared to the several hundreds of dollars that people might pay for the same trade through a regular stockbroker.

This shift in trading patterns has resulted in a significant change in the revenue structure of the Canadian investment industry. In 1997, revenue from fees and commissions generated by online investment totalled $630 million, compared to $1.47 billion racked up offline. But, by the end of 2001, it is expected that online charges will outpace offline fees, growing to $2.27 billion. The trend to online trading is even more pronounced in the U.S.; some 55 percent of trades done through Charles Schwab originate on the Internet.

What does this mean? For traditional stock brokerages, increased competition means lower commissions. Left unchecked, the situation will lead to strenuous cost-cutting, thereby putting many jobs at risk. Throughout the industry it also means massive investment in customer-based technology systems and far less investment in traditional retail operations. And in terms of careers, it means more opportunity for those involved in strategic implementation of Internet-based trading systems, and less for those who excel at traditional methods of dealing with customers.

Online banking is another industry that has been forever changed by the Internet. Just as dot-com gloom was settling in at the end of 2000, Statistics Canada noted that Canadians are taking to online banking with a vengeance. Two in ten Canadians are signed up for Internet banking, double the number from a year ago. And those who are registered for the service use it frequently: Six in ten (59 percent) report clicking on their account at least once a week, and three-quarters (77 percent) say they usually bank online at least once a month. These are just some of the findings noted in the annual marketing research report *Banking Services Delivery Study*, by Canadian Facts, a division of CF Group.

So some areas in the financial services industry have been massively affected by the Internet. What about other sectors? If online shopping is a bust, surely the idea of reaching consumers directly can't have much impact? Not so fast — if you dig down beneath the surface of the Internet to find out what is really going on, you will discover that, while people might not be buying groceries on the Internet, they are more than willing to buy other things online.

Consider travel: Signs abound that the Internet and e-biz are causing change throughout the travel sector. SouthWest Airlines, for example, books one out of every three tickets through its Web site, a pretty significant percentage. Other airlines report an even greater degree of online booking. This change in the way customers deal with organizations is causing havoc within the travel industry. Several travel associations report an alarming decrease in the number of travel agents because of the emergence of Internet booking systems.

It isn't just e-biz and e-commerce that are causing significant change. Entire sectors of the economy are undergoing a technological transformation imposed by the emergence of the Internet, with important impacts on business management and career opportunities.

Online retail? It might not be happening with consumer purchases, but for some companies and industries, a substantial number of orders are being managed through the technology of the Internet. Perhaps the Canadian leader in this regard is office supplier Grand & Toy. By mid-2001, they were well on their way towards their objective of at least 50 percent of their corporate customers using the Grand & Toy Web site for purchasing. This rewarded them with some major benefits of e-biz: lower transaction costs (hence, increased cost savings), more customer loyalty, and a sales staff that was able to spend more time selling instead of writing up routine orders.

The list goes on; there is no shortage of industries that have been profoundly affected by the connectivity afforded by the Internet. To think that the Internet and e-biz aren't having a major effect and providing significant opportunity is to deny reality.

Longer-Term Changes

We continue to believe that the Internet and the concept of e-commerce will, over time, cause significant and far-reaching change in many business sectors. As this change occurs, there will be plenty of upheavals in the business world and lots of new opportunity — for those who take the time to understand how the change will come about.

But we also believe, as we have stated from the beginning in our very first book, that the impact of the Internet is going to be felt over the long term, not the short term. After all, it took 30 or 40 years from the birth of the computer for companies to figure out how to take advantage of its technology. There is always a big delay between the introduction of something new and its ultimate impact; so it is with e-biz and the Internet.

The problem in the past few years has been that raging hype has led to a lot of short-term expectations. And that is the main point that you need to consider carefully if you are assessing your future business or career opportunities — *always, always think in the long term.*

Why is this so? For the simple reason that change takes time. People managed to convince themselves that when it came to the world of business, the Internet was somehow different — that people and companies would quickly adapt to new ways of doing business and that it would be easy to implement the technology. But as you will see in the next chapter, this wasn't the case.

QUESTION WHAT YOU READ!

We have come to realize over the years that the media often act like a herd of sheep, practising what we might call "herd journalism." Every once in a while, a report about some aspect of the Internet or e-biz is released, and the media pounce upon it with a fury — regardless of whether the story pumps up the Internet and e-biz or tears them down, regardless of whether the "facts" behind the story are statistically valid, and regardless of whether those facts or figures are even accurate. Sadly, they often just pick up a story and run with it — quality be damned — and manipulate it to fit the spin of the day.

The Dot-com Millionaire Media Love Affair

Media infatuation with "dot-com millionaires" was a problem throughout the years of dot-com excess, when we went through an intense period in which a certain spin was attached to the Internet. Suddenly, the idea of the "Internet IPO" made the Internet and e-biz look like a pot of gold, an instant way of achieving financial nirvana. Turn the page, and there was someone else worth a billion dollars!

You couldn't open a newspaper without reading a story about some kid who had cashed out for untold millions. It's difficult to fault the media, though, since they were only responding to a demand for Internet celebrities and heroes. Never mind that the valuation that made the individual "rich" was built on a house of cards, and that it was simply paper wealth, based on overly inflated stock values. Nor that the value would crash within a year to maybe a few hundred thousand dollars. The idea of dot-com millionaires fitted the media spin of the day, and the press embraced it with a passion. The Internet was booming, growth was exploding, people were getting rich — come and join the party!

Thankfully, that period of excess soon came to an end, with the market correction that cooled down high-tech stocks. But in its wake a new spin took over, one that was extremely discouraging about anyone's future in the wired economy. We began to see stories suggesting that maybe the Internet wasn't all it was cracked up to be. The media now seemed eager to destroy the allure of the Internet and technology, with as much eagerness as when they were building it up. We witnessed a flood of articles about dot-com flameouts, layoffs in the high-tech sector, and countless other technology problems. Certainly some were genuine issues, but one could also sense an undercurrent of "I told you so." There's the rub: The stories of dot-com millionaires were often unrealistic, but so too were many of those "Internet flameout" stories.

The Case of the Disappearing Web Users
Here's a good case of the unreality — and the unrealistic spin — of some media reports about the Internet and e-biz. This happened with a U.K. study that was released while we were writing this book.

Consider this headline in the *National Post*: "Youth Grow Bored with Internet: Web fails to change lives; British researchers claim Net is just a passing fad" (Monday, December 4, 2000). Oh, dear. Things must be pretty bad in the online world, you think. Reading the story, you would be convinced that the bright flame of the Internet was burning out as people turned off their computers and moved on to other things.

"In the United States almost 28 million people have stopped using the Internet, the study claimed. In Britain there could be more than two million former users." These numbers caught the readers' attention. This had to be a serious study, since lots of people from around the world were involved: ". . . according to the study conducted by 76 researchers from Britain, the United States, Denmark and Holland . . ." Seventy-six researchers — good gosh! The Internet must be closing down. A massive worldwide research study had confirmed this. What an astonishing story!

So began the media frenzy. News organizations — print, radio, and television — jumped on the story, each trumpeting the fact that 28 million people in the U.S. and 2 million in the U.K. had abandoned the Internet. The Manchester *Guardian*'s version of the story used a typical spin, noting that the Internet

. . . might end up looking in hindsight a lot like CB radio: initially a cult among specialists; a sudden, skyrocketing surge in popularity, and then, well . . . not

much, really. Mentioning one's email address at the better sort of party, it seems, might one day be as déclassé as loudly informing the assembled gathering of one's CB call sign.

The Internet as CB radio — here was a new angle! Every journalist that we dealt with over the next few days wanted to talk to us about the *fact* of declining Internet use. Certainly this affirmed that the Internet was only a fad, they suggested. Would we care to comment on the fact that the Internet was beginning to resemble CB radio?

But we sensed a few problems there, and decided to find out whether what was being reported worldwide in breathless headlines was in fact true. After all, the reporters were taking the study at face value, accepting without question that 30 million people were logging off in the U.K. and the U.S.

What we found was rather curious. First, the *National Post* had merely run, almost verbatim, an article that had appeared in the *Daily Telegraph* (which, incidentally, used the headline "Millions Log off the Internet to Join the 'Real World'"). Of interest to us was that no effort was made to put a Canadian spin on the story, although it appeared on the same day that a Statistics Canada study was released indicating that Internet use in Canada had increased significantly. Oh, dear.

We thought further about the figure of 28 million people logging off in the U.S. That's a stunning drop in usage at a time when there were an estimated 76 million Internet users. That meant that one out of every three Americans had decided to stop using the Internet. Suddenly. Twenty-eight million people out of 76 million — one out of three. Good gosh, this Internet thing must be in pretty bad shape!

All this was occurring during the period of massive dot-com flame-outs. The two events must be related, and surely the Internet was but a fad whose time had come. Many of the news articles duly made a point of linking the trends together.

The report in the *Guardian* caught our attention, since it commented that "According to a new survey, once-enthusiastic internet users are logging off in droves: 28 million people in the United States, and perhaps two million in the UK, now fall into the category of 'former internet users'." Note the phrase *new survey*. Where had this new survey come from? We were certainly curious, and our suspicions had been raised. Wouldn't you think, if one out of every three U.S. users of the Internet had quit the network, that other major research organizations might have noticed?

What we learned was fascinating, to say the least: The statistic behind the headline came from a press release issued a full 14 months earlier! How did we determine this? A story on the ZDNet U.K. news site indicated that the numbers came from a research report released by a U.S. company, and were in fact based on something released in 1999. "Figures just released by research firm Cyber Dialogue show that in 1999 30 million people in the US no longer used the Internet, describing themselves as 'former users'."

This led us to the Cyber Dialogue Web site (www.cyberdialogue. com), where we found the original press release, dated November 29, 1999. It had indeed come out a full year before the screaming headlines informed us that Internet use was declining at a rapid rate! Not only that, the numbers Cyber Dialogue used in its press release were from September 1999.

So, had 28 million Americans suddenly stopped using the Internet at the same time that the dot-com flameout was underway? Not quite — we seemed to be dealing with some rather old math. We were curious about where the numbers used by Cyber Dialogue came from, how they were arrived at, and the methodology behind the study. We never did receive an answer to our inquiries.

So who is Cyber Dialogue? Browse their site and you will see that they are an "eCRM [electronic customer relations management] company that provides businesses with an analytical solution for acquiring and retaining profitable customers" — certainly not an independent research organization. We don't intend to suggest that the figure of 28 million touted by Cyber Dialogue is tainted; we'll let you make your own judgement. But, good heavens, it's all quite curious.

Let's suppose we take the Cyber Dialogue number at face value. The press release comments that the number of adults who have tried the Internet and have discontinued use "totaled 27.7 million adults in September (1999), up from 9.4 million in early 1997." It then goes on to note that a third of these former users did not plan to log on again any time soon. Do the math: Does this mean that 28 million people suddenly abandoned the Internet? Not to us. It might mean that maybe 10 million people who had tried out the Internet found that it didn't appeal to them. That's fair — the Internet isn't for everyone, particularly older people. But that's a long way from 30 million people suddenly abandoning the network.

Then we found an interesting article in another U.K. publication, called *Revolution*, entitled "Vital Statistics" and dated December 13, 2000 (www.revolution.haynet.com):

Last week's media scare story was that the internet is losing audience and could be on the way out.

The stories were based on US figures for the number of former users put out by Cyber Dialogue. Of former users, many are university graduates who have not yet arranged their own connection, or workplace users who moved jobs.

How curious! So maybe 28 million people hadn't stopped using the Internet in 1999, but had merely lost access for a time while they were between locations. *Revolution* then went on to note that "One academic, Sally Wyatt, whose paper was quoted in support of the stories of doom, told me she was shocked at the fabrication of her opinions in the mainstream press."

And so we come full circle. Visit the Web site of the authors of the study (virtualsociety.sbs.ox.ac.uk/) and you'll find some interesting comments. They discuss the public whirlwind in which they found themselves, and how the world media turned their little report into the story "the Internet is dead":

As the storm unfolded, less careful coverage increasingly emphasized singular aspects of the research and built sensational stories around them. The Metro (a freebie paper for London tube travellers) apparently reported that 30 million people in the UK had stopped using the Internet. Some teenagers dropping off according to a US survey has been turned into the end of the Internet, the Internet is dead, no one is using the Internet anymore.

Not only that, but the media would sometimes call them with a preconceived story. "When Steve Woolgar refused (on BBC Radio Scotland 7.12.00) to concur with the proposal that 'there is no longer any point in buying a computer' he was told he was spoiling a good headline." (Excerpts are from the Virtual Society? Web site, virtualsociety.sbs.ox.ac.uk/reports/media.htm.)

What is funny about this situation is that the news media probably did much of the research for this story through the Internet. Here we have the media indicating that Internet usage is declining — and yet they are using the Internet to piece together their story, and basing their reporting on questionable numbers from a full 14 months earlier!

SOME CONTEXT

The point is this: Don't let the current state of gloom about the Internet and e-biz dissuade you from considering its future potential, particularly with respect to the job or career opportunities that it might present. It is all too easy to get caught up in extremes when it comes to the Internet and e-biz, and to think that either (a) there are no opportunities because they are having no impact, or (b) there are plenty of easy opportunities because this thing is so huge!

As we pointed out earlier, reality is somewhere in the middle. But, given the events of 2000–2001, right now there are probably more people who fall into the first category. Hence, it is important that you put these events into context; otherwise, it is too easy to become complacent about the potential of the Internet and e-biz.

Wild enthusiasm about the Internet and e-biz was followed by the high-profile collapse of many dot-com start-ups and a general pall over the high-tech sector, but that doesn't mean that opportunities don't exist. Also, you should put the failure of early-stage Internet businesses into context. Whenever a new or revolutionary technology arrives on the scene, there always seems to be a period of wild enthusiasm, followed by a significant reality check.

Putting Dot-com Collapse into Perspective

In 1840, there were 11,000 railway companies in England and Wales. By 1900, there were 11. This type of situation has happened many times. At the turn of the last century, there were thousands of automobile company start-ups and roaring enthusiasm for anything having to do with this new form of transportation. But, in the long run, only a few of these companies survived.

There have been more than 2,000 carmaking start-ups in this country since the first U.S. patent for an automobile in 1895, and the industry changed society irrevocably. Yet only three major U.S. auto companies survived.

"LET'S NOT GET CARRIED AWAY," *NEWSWEEK INTERNATIONAL*, FEBRUARY 12, 2001

The same thing happened with radio, television, and the airline industry. Each sector saw massive early enthusiasm, the establishment of hundreds of start-up companies, hundreds of thousands of eager investors — and subsequent collapse, as many of the early pioneers simply disappeared.

The point is this: As the Internet and e-biz move forward, opportunities will come and go. It's hard to predict which sectors will blossom and which will wither. Countless people are trying things out; testing new business models; attempting new ways of doing business; investing in new types of Internet infrastructure. Some will succeed and some will fail, but overall, over time, there will be more successes than failures. The Internet and the world of e-biz are a giant laboratory, one in which some things work out and others won't. And, as we will see in the next chapter, it is a world in which patience is a virtue.

And our fellow in the marina industry? He is definitely doing the right things with the Internet. He is aware of what is happening and on top of new business models that are being explored. He is cognizant of the potential challenges to his business, but he remains cautious about what he might do himself. That is perhaps the best approach to take; the fact of so many dot-com failures is good reason not to become complacent about the Internet and its potential impact on business and industry.

Chapter 2

Ten E-biz Myths Debunked

O NE PROBLEM WITH INTERNET AND E-BIZ HYPE IS THAT, OVER THE YEARS, many people came to accept as gospel some oft-repeated but factually suspect statements made by the media. The result is that certain myths have been drilled relentlessly into the heads of business executives.

HOW DO THESE MYTHS COME ABOUT?

Internet and e-biz myths become widespread because the online technology of the Internet — e-mail, discussion groups, mailing lists, and Web sites — allows the dissemination of information and ideas more rapidly than ever before possible. Add to this the dot-com investment mania, emerging greed, and a desire to grab a piece of the pie, and you have an explosive mix.

During the past several years, the public has displayed a remarkable capacity for quick acceptance of ideas, to the extent that the rapid adoption of an idea or "belief" came to be known as an "idea virus." To understand the weird and twisted impact of the Internet, you should know that the idea of the idea virus got turned into a book, word of which spread like wildfire online — because the book itself had become an idea virus! However, the author captures the essence of how Internet myths can come about:

It's a big idea that runs amok amongst a target audience. It's a fashionable idea that propagates through an entire section of the population. . . .

SETH GODIN, *UNLEASHING THE IDEAVIRUS* (WWW.IDEAVIRUS.COM)

Internet myths are idea viruses that have taken hold among the population. Repeated and exchanged, at first online and then through the media, they become like mantras. After they have been commented upon by enough people, they take on a life of their own. It has long been noted that if you repeat something over and over again, it becomes "true," regardless of whether the concept is real or not.

Take the idea of "Internet time," which is one of the myths that we discuss below. How did the phrase originate? Where did it come from, and why is it so widely accepted as fact? To put this particular phrase into perspective, we turned to Dow Jones Interactive, a massive online database of articles from tens of thousands of newspapers, magazines, journals, and reports. We did a careful month-by-month review, trying to determine when the phrase "Internet time" exploded onto the scene and entered the public consciousness. We found barely any mention of the phrase up until 1996. Any discussion of Internet time back then had to do with how to maximize use of your dial-up Internet connection.

But, even then, people were developing catchphrases about the Internet as they tried to describe the frenetic rate of evolution of the online world. If you were online then, you will remember such phrases as "20 years in human years is like one year on the Internet" or "time on the Internet is measured in months, not years." Other references to the speed with which things were happening online came to be popular, and were in widespread use throughout the Internet. Back then, we used many of those phrases ourselves in our speeches and presentations.

Then, in July 1996, both *Business Week* and *Time* magazine reported on the issue of Internet time. The interesting thing is that they weren't talking about rapid business-model change or the fact that companies were having to reinvent themselves on a regular basis. They were reporting on a significant new issue facing software companies. The Internet was speeding up the pace of software development so much that technology companies were scrambling to keep up. For example, Microsoft found its market in that period of dramatic upheaval.

Microsoft, already the ultimate hardcore company, is entering a new dimension. It's called Internet time: a pace so frenetic it's like living dog years — each jammed with the events of seven normal ones.

"INSIDE MICROSOFT: THE UNTOLD STORY OF HOW THE INTERNET FORCED
BILL GATES TO REVERSE COURSE," BUSINESS WEEK, JULY 15, 1996

And in Silicon Valley, the term was quickly becoming a buzz-phrase:

The one problem with this picture is that it is already outdated. In Silicon Valley, where I work, the running joke is that we're all on Internet time. That means that when a new idea gets established on the Internet, it has only a few weeks to flourish before it is eclipsed by another.

"IF YOU THINK THE INTERNET IS BIG NOW, WAIT UNTIL AUDIO AND VIDEO ARRIVE. OOPS, THEY'RE ALREADY HERE," *TIME*, JULY 8, 1996

Other publications quickly picked up on the concept that the software world was subject to significant change because of the Internet.

The fast-forward pace of software development and innovation brought on by the explosive growth of the global communications network has even generated a catch phrase: "Internet time," a twilight zone where programming milestones that used to take months or years to reach are passed in a matter of weeks.

"INTERNET TIME: IT FLIES AT WARP SPEED; MICROSOFT PROGRAMMER SCURRIED FOR EXPLORER 3.0," *SEATTLE POST-INTELLIGENCER*, AUGUST 12, 1996

Within a matter of weeks, it seemed, publications were picking up on the idea of Internet time, fed by catchy quotes and comments from folks within the technology world. "Internet time" was catching fire!

Yeah, managing in Internet time is big fun. Just ask those trying to survive it. CEO Kris Hagerman of BigBook Inc. says it's like driving on an icy mountain road — without lights. Marketing Director John Stuckey of ViewCall America Inc. complains that it's like playing in a soccer game with no time-outs. For CEO Doug Colbeth of Spyglass Inc., a single metaphor will not do: "It's like riding a motorcycle backward at 100 mph and trying to play chess where the pieces are changing and the board is moving."

"VICTIMS OF TIME," *PC WEEK*, DECEMBER 9, 1996

At first the phrase didn't seem to apply to much more than the rapid rate of technology development. That is, until 1998, when *Competing on Internet Time: Lessons from Netscape and Its Battle with Microsoft* was released. The book became a business bestseller and, overnight, much more credence was given to the concept of Internet time. With the book came the idea that it wasn't only software companies that were being affected by the speed of the Internet — *every* business would soon be hit by the rapid rate of change. The writing about Internet time began to reflect its purported speed, with articles penned in a style that almost left you breathless:

We're not talking hours. We're not talking minutes. We're not even talking seconds. No, to get to consumers in the hyperpaced (and cyberspaced) 1990s, it can conceivably take only milliseconds. Fast. Faster. Fastest. What an astounding, confounding and pulse-pounding time in which we live.

"RUSH HOUR," *ENTREPRENEUR*, FEBRUARY 1, 1998

Of course, the more the phrase was used, the more it became accepted. Everyone was talking and writing about Internet time. The business world was evolving so quickly that the idea of Internet time *must* be true! The catchphrase finally became solidified during the emergence of the dot-com investment phase. Our review of press releases from 1999 up to the dot-com collapse of 2000 reveals that an increasing number were taking the phrase to heart.

The PR community was grabbing on to Internet time. You had to raise money fast! You had to get into business fast! You had to be there first! The world is moving at Internet time, so you had better hurry! Press release after press release espoused the idea that these start-up venture capital and high-tech companies were operating on Internet time. Thus, of course, they were sure to succeed in the marketplace.

Brightspark employs a strong technology view, with emphasis on mentoring and a robust network of contacts and resources, to boost Canadian start-ups striving to get innovative products and services to the Internet market in an accelerated Internet time frame

"RIOCAN AND BRIGHTSPARK TEAM UP TO REVOLUTIONIZE CANADIAN INTERNET SHOPPING: NEW INTERNET BUSINESS CREATES CANADA'S FIRST BRICKS-AND-MORTAR/ INTERNET PARTNERSHIP," *CANADIAN CORPORATE NEWS*, FEBRUARY 1, 2000

Want to know what the future holds? Online "marketeers" attending today's @d:tech conference in London got a sneak peek at the future of marketing, and it's Oracle's newest offering: the E-Business Network, the first multi-channel Internet broadcast network. "In Internet time, there is no future and no past, just now followed by now followed by now," said Mark Jarvis, Oracle's senior vice president of Worldwide Marketing.

"ORACLE: 'E-CASTING' THE NET WIDER WITH E-BUSINESS NETWORK," *PR NEWSWIRE*, FEBRUARY 1, 2000

The mantra had been repeated so many times that people had come to accept it as fact. Is it true? We don't think so, as you will see below.

So it is with Internet myths. Some of them seem to emerge as quickly as algae bloom in a swimming pool. One day the water is clear and inviting; the next day, a few dark spots appear. And then, literally overnight, the algae take over the pool.

As you consider the future impact the Internet and e-biz might have on you and your business, or as you assess potential career opportunities, it is critical that you understand that many Internet mantras are just myths. That is why, in this chapter, we hope to give you an understanding that e-biz and the Internet may be a little more complex than you thought. And that means that the opportunities over the long term are perhaps more significant than you might have believed possible.

Let's get out the wrecking ball.

MYTH #1: E-BUSINESS IS EASY TO IMPLEMENT
REALITY: E-BUSINESS IS COMPLEX

Internet veterans and novices alike can visit SearchHound at http://webcart. searchhound.com to sign up for a trial account, and create their online store in only a few minutes.

"SEARCHHOUND.COM LAUNCHES NEW SHOPPING-CART SERVICE 'WEBCART,'"
BUSINESSWIRE, FEBRUARY 6, 2001

The press release above is typical of proponents of the myth that you can set up an e-business in a few minutes. The reality is that e-biz is far more complicated than most of them suggest, as is everything to do with the Internet. Many people promoted the idea, often backed up by advertising spin from the technology, dot-com, and Internet industry, that anything having to do with the Internet and e-commerce was "easy to do."

Set up a Web site, sit back, and watch the dollars flow in! Create a dot-com, generate some buzz, raise some venture capital, and get rich! Establish an Internet business with only a bit of work, and magic will happen! Create an "e-marketplace" and watch tens of thousands of companies sign on — barely any effort required!

Part and parcel of the "Internet is easy" spin were grand predictions about the rate at which the online marketplace would grow. For example, consider this prediction from 1994 about the size of the online shopping marketplace:

By 2000, Mr. Killen says, more than one-quarter of consumer shopping will be conducted remotely.
"RETAILING 2005: ELECTRONIC MALLS, VIRTUAL SHOPPING CARTS,"
CHRISTIAN SCIENCE MONITOR, DECEMBER 15, 1994

Over the past several years, we've been saying that we think that e-commerce, and many of the technological advances related to the Internet, will take 5, 10, 20, or even more years to unfold. Yet many people have come to think, because of the hype swirling around the Internet, that the implied changes and related benefits of the online world will happen overnight — because they believe that it is simple.

Well, many people have got it wrong, and obviously have realized far too late that the changes will happen much more slowly, because anything having to do with the Internet and e-commerce is tremendously difficult. Perhaps the root of the problem is that the technology of the Internet and e-commerce seem so easy. But the technology is the only easy part. Its implementation and execution have proven to be far more difficult.

"A Store in Minutes"

A good example of the "e-biz is easy" hype is found in the promotion of online shopping. We saw a situation in which people and organizations rushed into setting up online stores, lured by marketing literature from e-commerce and Internet service providers that promised, like the press release quoted earlier, that you could "set up a store in minutes."

Some of these services and this style of promotion still exist. Travel the Internet, explore the sales literature, and you'll be coached into believing that with just a few clicks, you'll be in business. At the Internet Store (www.internetstore.com), for example, you are assured that you can "create an online store or add a store to your existing site in a matter of minutes with just a few mouse clicks."

Similarly, at BuildStores (www.buildstores.com) you are told

BuildStores provides a free e-commerce platform for your business, either retailer or wholesale, to open your own online e-store, very quickly and easily with no risk. Take a Test Drive and setup your free e-store in a few minutes and sell your products online instantly to the world around the clock. No special skill or any additional software or tools is required.

The implication that it is easy to create an online store also appeared in media stories on a regular basis. The following quote is typical:

Even though setting up an Internet store — what's now dubbed "e-commerce" — isn't quite so easy as they make it look on TV, it's a heck of a lot easier and cheaper than opening a store anywhere else.

"VIRTUAL START-UP: HOW TO OPEN AN ONLINE STORE —
EVEN IF YOU'RE A TECH IGNORAMUS," *SUCCESS*, JANUARY 1, 1998

Sadly, the spin continues even today.

In the new category of Internet Application of the Year can be seen innovative solutions from some of the country's best known e-commerce software companies. These range from a simple-to-use solution to help businesses set up an online store within minutes and with minimal investments . . .

LIM CHONG, "MOVING FORWARD WITH E-COMMERCE,"
NEW STRAITS TIMES, SEPTEMBER 18, 2000

Yet, as we pointed out in our book *Selling Online*, trying to set up a store that quickly makes no sense whatsoever. The spin that you can create a store in "just minutes" hides the complex issues that are involved.

The fact is, in some cases, you can be up and running in a little more than thirty minutes — at least, in terms of having a Web site that lists your products.

But the thing is, out in the real world, no one sets up a retail store in thirty minutes.

The Internet and e-commerce aren't a game — they are something real. If you plan on taking your business to the Internet, you've got to approach this as a serious, important business initiative. You've got to plan, strategize, prepare, implement, execute, and follow up with the highest degree of professionalism and attention. You've got to think about issues like customer service and product fulfillment.

Otherwise, you are condemning yourself to playing a game in which the likelihood of losing is extremely high.

Setting up an online store is a business. You should never lose sight of that fact.

JIM CARROLL AND RICK BROADHEAD, *SELLING ONLINE*

Sure, it may be easy to create an online store on the Web. Some very sophisticated online services really do let you do it in only five minutes.

But that's the easy part, and in many ways, the fun part. But then there's the hard part, which involves the mundane, serious, and (perhaps for some) boring stuff — such as working hard to ensure that your store is noticed, and drawing up and executing an effective marketing campaign to make sure that people can find you. Then there are dealing with credit card fulfillment and payment issues, and following up on the inevitable credit card charges that come back to haunt you after the customer denies ordering a product — not to mention order fulfillment issues, and the big problems associated with customer support.

After getting involved with e-commerce, many an online retailer has quickly discovered that it involves a lot more than they bargained for. Sure, it's easy to build a shopping cart into a Web site, but if you don't do all the other things that go with it, then you are doomed to failure.

The B2B Bubble

Similar problems have come about because of lack of understanding of the complexity of B2B (business-to-business) marketplaces. Once many dot-com start-ups realized that online shopping was a bust, they figured they might be able to quickly implement systems that would transform the way goods and services are purchased within industries.

Thus was born the "e-marketplace," where buyers could post requests for goods and services and instantly receive responses from thousands of suppliers. Buyers would benefit from the lower cost of goods brought about by competition in the marketplace, and suppliers would benefit from additional market reach. If the media hype was to be believed, the entire history of business-to-business procurement would be transformed overnight.

The concept made sense and the software seemed straightforward. So the notion quickly grew that all you had to do was announce a "B2B vertical industry portal," and *poof!* It's magic: Business is transformed, and cost savings accrue!

Well, that didn't happen so quickly either. People involved in B2B initiatives discovered that the players in an industry needed a great deal of convincing to participate in their marketplace. While their online marketplaces could certainly win awards for effective Web design, they found that it took a huge amount of effort to integrate the technology of the B2B marketplace with the purchasing systems of participating companies.

Many B2B exchanges were failures because of the complexity of the task at hand.

. . . many companies sign on for E-procurement without anticipating the long road ahead. They dive into projects only to learn that E-procurement applications are limited in the types and scope of purchasing activity they address. Managing electronic catalogs with thousands of products, providing employees with the right mix of products and adequate information about them, and making it easy to search for items can also be tricky, requiring additional tools and threatening the efficiencies promised by moving purchasing to the Web. And integrating E-procurement applications with existing business systems, such as accounting and human-resources apps, can be more complex than planned.

"E-PROCUREMENT: PROBLEMS BEHIND THE PROMISE,"
INFORMATIONWEEK, NOVEMBER 20, 2000

What sunk B2B marketplaces? Many things, such as the limited functionality of many B2B software programs. There was also the complexity of integrating B2B applications with a company's internal human resources, inventory, accounting, and other systems. Many suppliers were suspicious that these marketplaces would lead to downward pressures on pricing. There was skepticism over benefits and cost savings, and concerns about losing relationships with trading partners by entrusting them to electronic ways of doing business. High training costs resulted from modifications to company purchasing systems, which also required substantial policy and process changes — not to mention fears about job cuts. All in all, plenty of extra weight was guaranteed to sink many such initiatives before they even left the dock.

The Simple Truth

Above all, what makes e-commerce difficult is the simple truth that *business is difficult.* To suggest that e-commerce is a magic pill that can make the complexity of running a business go away is simply wrong.

This leads to another key point: One of the main reasons why companies are slow to adapt to the complexity is because it takes a long time to implement a successful e-business strategy. A stand-alone Web site where sales can be made is easy enough to create, but before a business can really reap the benefits of e-commerce, training, integration, and business process issues have to be addressed.

Consider the amount of training a company has to do when a new e-business system is implemented. Many companies underestimate how important training is to the success of an e-business initiative. Take note of Dell Computers' experience when it deployed e-commerce software called Ariba Buyer, so that its employees could make purchases electronically:

Training is critical to gaining acceptance among users, yet it's often overlooked to the detriment of the project. Dell has deployed Ariba Buyer to 30,000 employees and has 3,000 frequent users, but the company wishes it had spent more time training users from the start. Although the company initially provided hour long training sessions, many users require additional support.

"E-PROCUREMENT: PROBLEMS BEHIND THE PROMISE,"
INFORMATIONWEEK, NOVEMBER 20, 2000

It also takes a long time to integrate e-commerce applications into accounting, inventory, and other computer systems. Along the way, companies often find that the e-commerce applications they are using have limited functionality, aren't user-friendly, and don't mesh well with their internal systems. Introducing a new e-business system company-wide also requires that the organization introduce new procedures, policies, and processes, which is easier said than done, especially in larger organizations with thousands of employees who are used to doing things a certain way.

Wrap it all up, and you'll realize that e-biz is very difficult. Even companies that have been at it for a long, long time, and who might be considered experts in the field, can find it hard to master all the myriad components of an online strategy. Too many elements of an online operation have to be operating to near perfection for everything to go smoothly.

Chapters.ca: A Case in Point

Let's come back to business-to-consumer (B2C) sales, and use a recent experience to put into perspective why e-commerce is so complex. Take Chapters.ca, the online portion of the Canadian bookstore chain, one of the earliest pioneers on the Canadian Internet retail scene. Within this organization there is probably far more experience in terms of what it takes to make an e-biz work than in any other organization in Canada. And yet it seems that even they still couldn't get it right.

Around the time this book was being prepared, one of the authors bought a Christmas present through the Chapters site. There were only two items in the order, and the Chapters Web site indicated that both were usually shipped within 24 hours. That didn't happen. The first item, a video, didn't ship until a few days after the order was placed. The second item, a Lego set, didn't ship until the author kicked up a stink some three weeks later.

What went wrong? Who knows? But the fact that a company four years into the e-commerce voyage was still struggling hints at the complexity that lies below the e-biz surface. And the problems we encountered aren't unique. You'd have to live in a cave not to realize that many online businesses have suffered during the past few years from substantial problems, and have been subject to huge numbers of complaints from their customers. These types of problems are not uncommon, and are symptomatic of the complexity of e-biz.

The Longer View: It's Always Been Hard

If you think about it, the complexity of e-business should come as no surprise, since implementing computer technology in the business environment is often a complicated task.

Consider this quote from 1971:

. . . far from simplifying technology or business, the computer has added complexity and imposed a constantly changing set of demands on scientists and managers. The integration of a mishmash of computer functions into a smooth-running system has turned out to be more difficult than anyone, including computer makers, ever expected.

"THE RECESSION FORCES A REAPPRAISAL," *BUSINESS WEEK*, JUNE 5, 1971

From the very earliest days of business systems, we have seen organizations struggle with the implementation of computer systems, their difficulties sometimes leading to complete havoc. Take this story from 1969:

In many a U.S. household last week, the story was the same. The morning mail had brought a bill for a charge-account or credit-card purchase, and in one way or another something was wrong. The customer was charged for something he had never bought. The amount was double what it should have been. The bill had been paid months ago. The common reaction: rage, often followed by helpless frustration . . .

"THE GREAT SNAFU," *NEWSWEEK*, SEPTEMBER 15, 1969

The result is that computer pioneers have long joked about what they call "Westheimer's Rule": To estimate the time it takes to do a task, estimate the time you think it should take, multiply by two, and change the unit of measure to the next highest unit. Thus, we allocate two days for a one-hour task.

The information technology landscape is littered with the remains of projects that were not implemented within the projected time frame, could not deliver what was promised, and often turned into unmitigated disasters. The bottom line when it comes to any computer technology is this: It takes a lot of time and effort to design and implement a smoothly running information technology system — of any type, for any company.

So why should e-biz and Internet applications be any different? They aren't, and to suggest anything different is an out-and-out lie. We leave you with this story:

Early this year, Thomas & Betts Corp., a $2.5 billion electrical parts maker in Memphis, blamed problems with a new Internet-based order-management system for a 50% drop in profits in the fourth quarter of last year. The home-grown mainframe system also cost the company another $42 million in order and shipping disruptions. In the following quarter, the company spent $11 million on customer service, extra freight costs and other measures to make up for ongoing system crashes and backlogs.

"RECIPE FOR DISASTER: COMPANIES DON'T LEARN FROM PREVIOUS I.T. SNAFUS,"
COMPUTERWORLD, OCTOBER 30, 2000

MYTH #2: E-BUSINESS IS CHEAP TO IMPLEMENT
REALITY: E-BUSINESS IS EXTREMELY EXPENSIVE

80 percent of all software development efforts are 200 percent over budget . . . we're in an industry where success is the exception.

WAYNE BECKMAN OF INFORMATION CONCEPTS (A RESCUE OPERATION
FOR COMPANIES STRUGGLING WITH INTERNET SOLUTIONS),
QUOTED IN THE *WASHINGTON POST*, SEPTEMBER 20, 2000

The myth that e-business is easy fuels another myth — that e-business is inexpensive.

A Web Shopping Cart Is Not an E-business

Another aspect of the attitude that e-biz is easy came with what we call the "shopping-cart mentality." If it's easy to create an online store, it must be inexpensive — or so went the line of reasoning. As online shopping emerged, it was very easy for people to build the technology to support a "shopping cart" in a Web site. The programming was straightforward: Show a product, a description, and a price, and let the customer generate an order by clicking a few buttons. Extremely easy, and inexpensive.

It's true — it doesn't cost much to bring in a Web server, do a bit of programming, and set up a Web site. This led to the spin that the "barriers to entry" were low because the technology cost was low. The idea was promoted that a world market was waiting for anyone who could afford the modest cost of setting up a Web site.

And its global reach is not just for the IBMs of the world. Because the price of entry onto the Web is relatively low, a corner flower shop, for example, has the potential to become a global flower powerhouse virtually overnight with the right kind of approach.

BOB WEHLING (SENIOR VICE-PRESIDENT, ADVERTISING, PROCTER AND GAMBLE),
"THE FUTURE OF MARKETING: WHAT EVERY MARKETER SHOULD
KNOW ABOUT BEING ONLINE," *VITAL SPEECHES*, JANUARY 1, 1996

But what everybody discovered over time is that a Web site is not the same thing as a business. Take a look at Canadian Tire: When they announced their e-commerce initiative in the fall of 2000, they took abuse in the media for having invested some $20 million in the project. How could a company spend so much money on a Web site? It isn't even a particularly pretty one, some critics have said.

This response is typical of the narrow thinking around e-biz. The portion of the Canadian Tire site that people see online is just a tiny part of the company's e-biz venture. Where did Canadian Tire spend most of their money? For that answer we turned to Mark Foote, the company's CEO. His answer should be required reading for anyone even thinking of getting involved with e-commerce. Mr. Foote responded to our e-mail query as follows:

We didn't spend $20 million on a web site. We spent $20 million to start a business.

At Canadian Tire, our investment could be broken down into roughly 4 categories: site development, infrastructure implementation, business process design and content. Each component was a material portion of the $20 million, say about 25% per.

On site development per se, Canadian Tire wanted to minimize costs and improve speed-to-market. To help us do that, we took a risk by purchasing an e-commerce platform that we felt was excellent for e-tailing from Blue Martini software. The investment got us a long way towards having the e-store ready quickly because out of the box, it was an excellent platform.

Beyond our investment to acquire the software, the site's development expenses were really based on the customization to the platform caused by the kinds of benefits that we wanted our customers to enjoy — online Canadian Tire money as one example. If all you wanted to do was bring up a website, even with a commercially rigorous e-commerce platform like Blue Martini or IBM's Web Sphere products, even a big company can get away with 2–3 million using platforms instead of writing the whole thing from scratch.

The real money (and the real complexity) is in the other costs, not the site.

You spend big time on infrastructure and the bigger you are, the more you'll spend. If you don't have direct-to-home distribution, which most tradi-tional retailers don't, you have to establish new distribution capabilities and transportation tracking systems. On the technology side, you need to estab-lish the production, development and testing infrastructure for the site's oper-ations, the call centers for customer interactions etc. The issue you have if you are an established business is that, given you can't easily forecast volumes, and given that you have an established brand to protect, you tend to spend heavily because you do not want to have any problem reacting to demand if it materializes.

Business process design is time consuming and costly. For a retailer used to sending 53' trailers to stores and not having direct interactions with customers centrally, there is a lot of process design work to do. Most of your established business processes don't apply.

And internet e-commerce brings new issues to fairly simple business processes such as online fraud protection that has to be added to your credit management systems. You have to develop new systems to allocate inventory, everything down to how customer relations deals with an email complaint.

Finally, there's content. If there's any area where you will spend more than you ever imagined it's in content development and management.

All the product shots, descriptions, associations, selling features, related products, step-up products and then everything in two languages. Rarely will the site differentiate you (positively) but the quality of your content sure can.

The site itself is a fairly simple issue. I would say conservatively, that 75% of the cost in starting the business is the stuff that is behind the site. And as stated, if your site doesn't have a lot of unique features, you can get away with relatively little using excellent and robust off-the-shelf e-commerce platforms that come packaged and ready to go with product search, call center integration, credit authorization and sophisticated data mining systems. If you don't have to modify them much you're off to the races pretty quickly.

Putting everything in place behind the scenes, that's a different story.

Hidden Costs of B2B

The belief that e-biz is inexpensive has shown up in the hype around B2B and e-marketplaces. Once it became apparent that online shopping was turning out to be a bust, B2B was promoted as a revolutionary new business method that would forever transform entire industries — quickly, easily, and cheaply.

It *was* easy to create B2B Web sites, since many of them are just like shopping carts. It was straightforward, piece-of-cake programming, and therefore inexpensive. But many B2B initiatives didn't bother with a critical aspect that was needed to make them work: integration into the back-end systems and day-to-day business processes of participating companies.

As we will see later in this book, implementing the many different aspects of e-biz is probably one of the most complicated projects the corporate sector has ever set out upon. And a complex process is an expensive one. That is the key point.

The Productivity Paradox

There has long been a significant lag between the introduction of new computer technology and the benefits that result from its implementation. And there is a big delay between the emergence of new technologies and when companies establish new ways of doing business that are based upon it.

Almost as soon as computer technology was invented, phrases of promise and potential filled the news. As far back as 1954, the *Financial Post* noted that "if electronic devices are efficiently used the saving in personnel will be matched by increased efficiency." Such prose was typical; two years later, in a hopeful article titled "Office Automation Need Not Cost Millions," the same publication liberally sprinkled about the catchphrases of the office automation revolution: "reduction of work"; "improvement in efficiency"; "relief of tedium"; "elimination of error"; "descending office costs"; "new effectiveness."

Thus were born the mantras of the computer era as business publications began to promote the bottom-line productivity improvement that was just around the corner. Computers would change the very nature of the office and ease our frustrations. They would allow new ways of working, and would permit organizations to reinvent themselves.

Well, that didn't happen right away. Companies discovered that there was a big lag between the arrival of a technology and its successful deployment. By the 1990s, they were wondering where the value from the investment was. "American companies spent $1 trillion on computer systems in the last decade with almost no gain in productivity," noted *Newsweek* in 1995. Reports began to circulate that even though huge sums of money were invested in information technology in the eighties and previous decades, the productivity improvement was only 0.7 percent. Where was the missing efficiency, they wondered. Respected publications such as *Business Week*, *Forbes*, and the *Harvard Business Review* undertook lengthy essays and analyses trying to understand what was going wrong.

Within only a few more years, however, the business sector had again changed its tune — it was finally enjoying the productivity improvements of the computer age. Having spent many years implementing sophisticated office technologies, it was realizing that the long-promised efficiencies were finally coming about. No less a luminary than Alan Greenspan weighed in, trumpeting that the economy was at last witnessing the productivity improvements of computer technology within the workplace:

. . . innovations in information technology — so-called IT — have begun to alter the manner in which we do business and create value, often in ways that were not readily foreseeable even five years ago.

ALAN GREENSPAN, CHAIRMAN, BOARD OF GOVERNORS OF THE
FEDERAL RESERVE SYSTEM, FROM TESTIMONY BEFORE THE UNITED STATES
CONGRESS JOINT ECONOMIC COMMITTEE, JUNE 14, 1999

Think about what happened here. It took from 10 to 40 years for companies to figure out how to implement technology internally in order to change the way they worked. And they spent a heck of a lot of money doing so. Along comes the Internet, and in the initial excitement, there were those who thought it would be easy and inexpensive to implement. But there has always been a massive delay between the early promise of technology and achievement of its benefits in the corporate workplace — and significant expense to realize those benefits. Companies have long known that implementing technology is expensive, so why should the Internet and e-biz be any different?

MYTH #3: YOU CAN BUILD A PROFITABLE INTERNET BUSINESS ON COOKIE CRUMBS
REALITY: ONLINE CUSTOMERS ARE EXTREMELY HARD TO COME BY

Together with the buzz that the Internet and e-biz would be easy and inexpensive came the belief that you could build an Internet business with only a very small percentage of the market. Instead of going after the whole cookie, the idea was to go after the crumbs.

This attitude was most apparent in the spin that reaching potential customers on the Internet would be such a low-cost proposition that it would not take much to attract enough customers to build a profitable business. Consider this quote from a 1997 issue of *USA Today*:

For the reach that is afforded by the Internet, it by far is the most cost-effective marketing method ever devised. Moreover, Internet presence is much less expensive than traditional advertising. For instance, the same ad that costs $200 a day in a newspaper would be pennies a day on the Internet.

"TOP 10 EXCUSES FOR IGNORING THE INTERNET," *USA TODAY*, JANUARY 1, 1997

Articles such as these implied that you could spend pennies a day on the Internet and achieve the same success that you would have with more expensive traditional advertising. From that belief, companies made the leap of faith that they could quickly gain enough Web-site visitors to build a successful business. Consider the founders of Pets.com, who saw a huge potential marketplace:

I am excited to be part of the Pets.com team, a company that addresses a category I am passionate about. This is a $23 billion market in the U.S. alone with no e-commerce leader. My goal is to establish Pets.com as the clear winner.

"FORMER REEL.COM CEO JOINS PETS.COM," *BUSINESS WIRE*, MARCH 5, 1999

As framed by Pets.com's business plans, the cookie crumbs looked so infinitesimally small that they seemed easy to achieve. Many companies looked at the $23 billion pet-care/pet-food market and thought that, if they could grab just a small part of it through the Internet, they were set to win. They said to themselves, "Gee, if we can grab only 5 percent, that's a big number. And surely 5 percent can't be too difficult to achieve."

The problem was, while 5 percent *seemed* like a tiny number, it proved to be a massive challenge, given the efforts required to build a successful online brand, and the reluctance of consumers to shop online. It is going to take many years for even 5 percent of the pet market to come online, let alone for us to see one company manage to dominate the channel. It is reasoning like this that led to the failure of so many dot-coms. In industry after industry, people succumbed to the belief that it would be easy to thrive by grabbing just a small share of the marketplace.

"Cookie-crumb" thinking came to dominate other aspects of e-biz and are still quite prevalent today. They are often framed in terms of potential cost savings rather than percentage share of a marketplace. For example, a company might think about the cost savings that could be achieved with an e-billing application in terms like this: "Every time someone chooses to receive their statements electronically, that's a little bit of postage, a little bit of paper, and a little bit of transaction processing that we have avoided. If we can convince 10,000 people to sign up, the annual savings on postage alone could come to about $50,000 a year. Get 100,000 online, and that's half a million dollars!"

It looks like it should be easy to achieve massive cost savings with e-biz, but it isn't — as e-billers are already discovering. Our imaginary company talks about saving half a million dollars if they can get 100,000 users to sign up. There lies the problem: How do you get those 100,000 people to participate? Some areas of e-biz take effort, time, and money to convince people and companies to join in. Indeed, signing those people up could conceivably cost more than the potential half-million dollars in money saved. Cost savings won't come about unless users flock to the service, the same way that B2C (business-to-consumer) revenues won't happen if customers don't start buying online in large numbers. That is why it is important that anyone involved with e-biz always be cautious about cookie-crumb thinking.

MYTH #4: PEOPLE'S BEHAVIOUR WILL CHANGE OVERNIGHT
REALITY: OLD HABITS ARE EXTREMELY HARD TO BREAK

Far from being merely a technological issue . . . putting e-commerce in place within companies is crucially about understanding and managing the hopes, fears and motivations of key members of the work force. Failure to get this right creates an enemy within, a fifth column of employees intent on protecting their own interests at the expense of the company's.

"BUSINESS-TO-BUSINESS ONLINE: THE TOUGH REALITIES," *PUBLISHING TECHNOLOGY REVIEW*, JUNE 1, 2000

It isn't just the complexity of the undertaking that gets in the way of making e-biz work. Perhaps one of the most powerful forces slowing down development of the Internet and e-biz is people's natural resistance towards change. Nowhere is this more apparent than in the often glacial rate at which they tend to change their behaviour and attitudes towards the Internet.

Why? The basic reason is that *most people are fundamentally resistant to change.* Regardless of how compelling the reason to change, many will hold back simply because they do not want to change. In fact, many people fight change in order to protect their turf.

This is, of course, nothing new. Business executives have long struggled with promoting change within organizations, whether it has to do with new ways of working or with overall organizational culture. The Internet and e-commerce represent dramatic change — perhaps some of the most fundamental change that has ever been thrust upon the world of business. And that isn't an overstatement, if you take the long-term view.

People don't change so fast. That's human nature. Everyone is in favor of change in the abstract, but when it comes to things that will specifically alter people's lives, they freak out. What's more, people don't change their reading or shopping behavior all that fast.

MARC ANDREESSEN, FOUNDER OF NETSCAPE,
QUOTED IN *FAST COMPANY*, FEBRUARY 2001

Consumer Habits

Consider, for example, how slow consumers have been to take to online shopping. Why? Having heard about the problems that plague many online retailers, a lot of buyers are unconvinced that it's a better alternative to traditional shopping. Others have concerns about security. Others resist paying the high delivery fees — many would rather walk down to their local store and save themselves the five-dollar shipping charge. And besides, many of them *like* shopping in the real world. Why should they give it up?

Companies selling on the Internet need to appreciate that consumers won't embrace online shopping overnight. Many businesses failed to grasp this concept, and as a result developed massively unrealistic expectations about the potential for online shopping. They are fooling themselves if they think, as many did a few years ago, that retail stores and shopping malls will go out of business immediately as consumers move all their buying to the Internet.

Employee Habits

Just as difficult as changing consumer behaviour is changing the way a company works. E-biz involves significant changes in the way that people work day by day, and it isn't something that can occur overnight. The experiences of many an e-biz pioneer certainly demonstrate this fact.

Oracle itself has been through the huge learning curve of becoming an e-business. As a company that bet its own business on the internet five years ago, we underwent a huge program of change throughout the organization. Dismantling fiefdoms and overcoming resistance is always a challenge.

"A VERY MODERN REVOLUTION," *NEW STATESMAN*, JANUARY 22, 2001

How does change affect the success of e-commerce implementation in organizations? Well, consider the opportunity of e-procurement, a topic we will explore in more depth later in this book. (It involves the online purchase of goods or services by a company.) E-procurement is a perfect example of an e-biz application that makes absolute sense from a strategic perspective. Is it being adopted as quickly as it could be? No.

In some industries, things seem to be going so slowly with e-procurement that one can sense deep frustration in the crowd who are pushing this type of solution. Day after day, they are busy trying to sell what seems to be a slam-dunk e-biz application — it offers cost savings, it's quite straightforward, and it's one of the less difficult e-biz solutions to start out with. Their arguments are extremely compelling, but they are meeting with only limited success. We suspect that they are silently screaming inside, "What's wrong with you people? There are cost savings on the table! You can save money by deploying this stuff! It's a no-brainer! Why aren't you doing this!?"

There sit the accountants, financial officers, purchasing managers, senior executives, and regular staff of corporate organizations, in companies large and small, who are cautious and careful in their approach to the ways of the world. Sure, they are reading about e-procurement, they have heard people talk about it at industry conferences, and they know that it seems to offer much potential, but they aren't prepared to jump on it. Why? Because they need a lot of convincing that this is the way to go. They need education, direction, and in-depth understanding of what it is about. They're comfortable with the way they, and the companies they work for, have been doing business for the last 25 years. Why should they go out on a limb and get involved with some new-fangled technology thing? Everything they read in the media questions the validity of the concept of e-business. They certainly don't want to take a risk!

Not only that, but they are busy with their many day-to-day activities. They are often deeply involved in crisis management, and can focus little energy on new, bold initiatives. Who has time for new things? Many of those who could be instrumental in the success of e-procurement are not involved in strategic activities — they are simply day-to-day "firefighters." They are complacent, and suspicious. What is wrong with current ways of doing business? they ask.

After all, their purchasing activities have been built on human relationships. They've got a long history of dealing with certain people in certain organizations, and they know their nuances, their needs, and the best way to cut a deal with them. Why should they get involved with this new way of doing business, when the current way works fine? It's a good question. And they need agreement and support from their senior management, since no one likes to take a risk. Yet senior management are not forthcoming with that support, because they too are resistant to change (as we note below in Myth #5). In the absence of direction regarding options, they just ignore the entire issue. The result? Natural resistance to change slows things down.

The problem comes down to human behavior, says Gary Dennis, senior vice president in investment banking at Robert W. Baird & Co. "People don't want to change," he says. They won't use a new Web site when they've worked the phones and personal relationships so well for so long, he says.

"DODGING ICEBERGS," *INTERACTIVE WEEK,* JANUARY 17, 2001

Why is there such reluctance to change? Suspicion is one of the main reasons. As we discuss later in this book, cost savings from using the Internet and e-commerce are one of the most important opportunities online. Businesses are discovering that they can change their information processes by using the Internet and save money at the same time. But these cost savings have led to reports of future layoffs as Internet-based re-engineering takes hold. General Electric, for example, told employees in February 2001 that they expected that utilizing the

Internet for business purposes would enable them to cut some 11,000 jobs. Is that kind of statement likely to get staff excited about the Internet? Is it going to put them in a mood to support e-biz activities wholeheartedly? Do employees at other organizations read such pronouncements and then next day march back to work eager to move forward with e-commerce projects?

Let's put the issue in context, using a real situation we found ourselves involved in. Grand & Toy, a major Canadian office-supply chain, figured that it needed to adopt a new, Internet-based customer order system in order to achieve the cost savings promised by e-commerce. But in order to make it a success, customers would have to readily adopt the technology. And who deals with those customers? The sales force, a group of people whose livelihood depends upon their relationships with the customers.

Would a typical salesperson want to embrace this e-commerce technology? Not a chance, for some of them! They view the technology with a huge degree of suspicion. After all, if they manage to convince their customers to order directly through the Web site, they won't be needed any more. Supporting e-biz could put them out of a job! They've read about planned layoffs resulting from the efficiencies to be found with e-commerce. There isn't a snowball's chance in hell that they'll support the effort.

Does Grand & Toy intend to let people go — is that the objective of this e-commerce application? No, their goal is to free up sales staff from the routine day-to-day paperwork that goes with order taking. The theory goes — and it is a good one — that when salespeople aren't kept busy writing up orders with the customer, they can work harder to sell higher-value products, provide additional services, and generally increase the revenue from that customer. So to make the e-commerce project a success, the company has to spend a great deal of time with its sales force, selling them on the plan, seeking their buy-in, and pushing the effort forward. All of this slows down implementation of the e-commerce project, and makes it more difficult to implement.

The bottom line? Behavioural change does not happen quickly. Both within and outside the organization, people are hugely resistant to change.

MYTH #5: E-BIZ VISIONS ARE READILY ACCEPTED
REALITY: CULTURAL CHANGE DOES NOT HAPPEN OVERNIGHT

Consumers and employees are not the only people resistant to change; so is management. To succeed in e-biz, however, an organization requires leadership and vision at the top. That is why so many established companies have been slow to weave the Internet into their operations, or haven't grabbed on to the new business models and potential that it presents.

From what we have seen so far, companies are often reluctant to adopt the Internet quickly because their leadership is reluctant. Throughout the corporate world there are many senior executives who just aren't ready to embrace e-biz and the Internet. And in the absence of leadership, e-biz is dead in its tracks. This is a different aspect of change than what we discussed in Myth #4. Yes, it takes time for consumers and employees to change their day-to-day behaviour. But it also takes time for people — and in particular, leaders — to envision a future that involves e-biz and, hence, accept new ways of doing business.

Many corporate organizations, large and small, are rather set in their ways. They've built successful markets, developed effective distribution strategies, and established long-term customer and supplier relationships. The Internet and e-commerce can fundamentally change every aspect of how they operate. Are they going to jump up and embrace them overnight? Not a chance. Senior executives in every industry, in every company, have been cautious in their analysis of Internet and e-biz opportunities; they're reluctant to move forward without giving the situation a great deal of thought. After all, the Internet can cause pretty dramatic change, and one false move could spell disaster.

Consider the dilemma faced by insurance CEOs. They see that some consumers seem to be readily embracing the Internet as a tool by which to learn more about insurance. (Yes, even though many are slow to embrace change, there are always others who are well ahead of the curve!) They are starting to visit Web sites that allow them to do a form of comparison shopping with respect to their insurance needs. And there are new competitors on the horizon who will sell insurance policies directly to these consumers through the Internet.

The CEOs are facing a big e-dilemma. They can choose to establish Web sites to sell insurance policies directly to their customers. But if they do so, they risk the wrath of insurance brokers and agents, who will view such a move as an assault on their livelihood. Many insurance agents have what is known as "non-captive" status — that is, they represent products from a number of different insurance companies. It's a good bet that these non-captive agents would decide not to sell products from the offending company.

So, what e-biz decisions do the CEOs make? Most certainly they will decide not to rush into an online strategy, because it could have such dire consequences. So they put the issue on the back burner for a while and move on to other things. This isn't surprising; trying to figure out an appropriate e-biz strategy in this type of situation is very difficult.

The corporate sector's attitude of caution has only been reinforced by the dot-com collapse. Because they have witnessed a wide-ranging number of business strategy failures, many senior executives today are even more cautious about e-biz than they were before. All that water under the bridge means that there is less courage to take dramatic steps forward.

Changing Corporate Culture

To make e-biz work, organizations need massive commitment and vision at the top. If a CEO isn't prepared to provide the leadership necessary for moving forward, an e-biz initiative is going to make no progress whatsoever.

E-business typically needs to be driven from the top, and it is often a painful process and one that leads to major transformation throughout the entire organisation. However, there is often resistance to the radical developments in working practices and culture that inevitably follow.

"A VERY MODERN REVOLUTION," *NEW STATESMAN*, JANUARY 22, 2001

Even organizations that have witnessed massive e-biz-induced change find that dealing with resistance to change is a complex process. Once again, the barriers to success with e-biz are not technical, but cultural.

The CEO of Charles Schwab, a company that has been massively transformed by e-biz, admits that trying to encourage the organization to move forward and embrace e-biz was one of the most difficult things he had to do.

Corporate culture is still a top-down-driven phenomenon at most companies. In making the transition to the New Economy, managers and employees are going to look to the chief executive. In fact, a new study by Mercer Management Consulting Inc. concludes that overhauling a company's culture is the No. 1 requirement for implementing a successful Internet strategy, and it's a charge that must be led by the CEO.

MICHAEL J. MCDERMOTT, "MANAGING THE TRANSITION FROM BRICKS TO CLICKS," *BUSINESS OPPORTUNITIES HANDBOOK: ONLINE* (WWW.BUSOP1.COM/BRICKS.HTML), AUGUST 1, 2000

Organizational sclerosis has been directly responsible for the failure of many e-biz initiatives. Nowhere has this been more apparent than with the widespread failure of B2B marketplaces. A number of dot-coms set up e-commerce initiatives in the expectation that thousands of businesses would suddenly move to adopt this new business model. What they failed to appreciate is that such a shift will take years to occur, because it takes a long time for companies to accept new ways of doing business. And so, the dot-coms collapsed.

Consider the experience of Efdex, a B2B market site that focused on the global food and drink industry. Their business plan called for them to sign up 40,000 food and beverage companies to do their purchasing electronically, their plan being to link buyers in restaurants with suppliers. They managed to sign up only about 2,000, burned through their $60 million (U.S.) in funding, and ended up going out of business, because the companies didn't sign on to their concept as quickly as they had hoped. And, obviously, most didn't buy into the concept at all.

Many organizations are extremely set in their ways of conducting business. And they view the radical new business models and ideas arising from the emergence of the Internet with a great degree of suspicion. Even those that want to change find problems bringing it about. Covisint is the highest-profile B2B site, and sponsored by leading car manufacturers around the world. A year after it was announced, it is still barely off the ground.

. . . the online exchange remains more of a dream rather than a reality for many in the industry. . . . Linking automakers and suppliers together to create a business-to-business (B2B) network has taken longer than many in the industry initially imagined. "B2B takes time. It takes time to sort out the processes internal to their companies, to get comfortable with using their tools," Alice Miles, Ford's top official at Covisint, said in an interview.

REUTERS, "COVISINT — A YEAR LATER — STILL A PROMISE," FEBRUARY 28, 2001

We leave you with this thought, which neatly brings together all of our myths so far:

Anyone who has tried to create a culture, however, knows it can't be done on Internet time. Cultures aren't designed. They simmer; they fester; they brew continually, evolving their particular temperament as people learn what kind of behaviour works or doesn't work in the particular company. The most critical

*factor in building a culture is the behaviour of corporate leaders, who set exam-
ples for everyone else (by what they do, not what they say).*

ART KLEINER, "CORPORATE CULTURE IN INTERNET TIME,"
STRATEGY & BUSINESS, FIRST QUARTER, 2000

Notice the reference to Internet time — a handy segue to our next myth.

MYTH #6: YOU MUST ACCELERATE YOUR BUSINESS TO RUN ON "INTERNET TIME"
REALITY: SPEED KILLS

The much-hyped concept of Internet time is one of the biggest fallacies
promoted during the past several years. Consider this quotation:

*Companies that can't live in Internet time, that can't get product to market
faster than ever, that can't rewrite a business model at the drop of a hat —
hardly stand a chance.*

"VICTIMS OF TIME," *PC WEEK*, DECEMBER 9, 1996

The exact opposite seems to have happened — those dot-coms that
rushed around changing their business models every other week have
now all but disappeared. The slow and steady, old-economy companies
are the ones that are still around.

Based upon experience so far, one could almost believe that
"Internet time" is a synonym for "bad business decisions." In the rush
to embrace e-commerce and e-business, many businesses neglect important business fundamentals, and that can do tremendous damage.

There's nothing wrong with e-biz and the Internet — you just have
to keep your sanity as you deal with it. As Judith Hurwitz, an *InformationWeek* columnist, puts it, "If you have any doubts about taking this
extra time, just remember the maniac driver who passed you on the
highway the other day — and how good it felt to see him pulled over
by the police a few miles down the road." ("In E-Business Planning,
Speed Kills," *InformationWeek*, June 12, 2000)

The Pace Is Picking Up

*We are moving from a world in which the big eat the small to a world in which
the fast eat the slow.*

KLAUS SCHWAB, PRESIDENT OF THE WORLD ECONOMIC FORUM,
QUOTED IN *THE OBSERVER*, FEBRUARY 4, 2001

If it's true, the statement above should cause alarm. But let's explore the problem in a bit more depth. What is Internet time all about? The spirit of the idea is best found in this quotation:

Silicon Valley entrepreneurs, who often call themselves evangelists, speak with quasireligious fervor of "Internet time" — the apocalyptic sense of urgency caused by the fleeting half-lives of products and business plans.

TIM RACE, IN *INDUSTRY STANDARD*, AUGUST 20, 1999

We live in a world in which the pace of technological and business change is definitely speeding up. Indeed, in our book *Lightbulbs to Yottabits*, we predicted that slow industries will be forced to become fast industries:

. . . the rapid rate of change, fuelled by the connectivity of the Internet, will come to mean that many industries, which have luckily not had to innovate too quickly, are going to find that luxury disappear.

For a long time, there has been a dichotomy in the economy. Certain industries, such as pharmaceuticals, hi-tech (including computers, software, and telecommunications), fine chemicals, and other industries, have felt the effect of the nano-cycle. They've been forced to operate extremely fast by constantly innovating and developing new sources of products or services, and hence new sources of revenue, on a regular and ongoing basis.

Many other industries have avoided the "fast-economy" so far. These include industries like banks and other financial services, airlines, media, entertainment, general manufacturing, and real estate. The list of industries that have not yet been subject to the rigours of constant, relentless innovation goes on.

Yet . . . this is no longer the case. There is a new type of nano-cycle looming on the horizon, one that doesn't involve technological evolution, but does involve the technology of the Internet. Basically, the Internet, in wiring the world's economy together, is going to cause new business models to develop at a very rapid rate, which will subject each and every business on the planet to a world of constant, ongoing change.

JIM CARROLL AND RICK BROADHEAD, *LIGHTBULBS TO YOTTABITS: HOW TO PROFIT BY UNDERSTANDING THE INTERNET OF THE FUTURE* (1999)

The business world is going faster, but "Internet time" is a crock.

Real Change Takes Time

It takes a lot of time to make Internet and e-biz applications work. And if people are naturally resistant to change, and hence resistant to Internet initiatives that might change their jobs, then things will be even slower still. Also, many companies in many industries are not prepared for rapid adoption of the new business models being promoted. There is a big gap between the pace of innovation and people's ability to cope with that innovation. So it is with the Internet and e-biz, which leads to a basic, undeniable fact that is extremely relevant as you assess your opportunities in the wired economy: *Everything about the Internet takes longer than you think.*

There is no doubt that many people *wish* the world would operate on Internet time. Those involved in the high-tech community, Internet start-ups, and e-commerce companies are intensely frustrated that the world won't move as quickly as they can. Many early failures with the Internet and e-biz probably happened because people didn't realize that the prevalent assumption — that businesses must speed up to run on some kind of super-fast Internet time — is simply not true.

Some Things Need to Move Slowly

Not only is the concept of Internet time a fallacy, but there is also some question as to whether organizations need to accelerate *all* the aspects of their operations. Many procedures within the business world do seem to move slowly, and they could be perceived as barriers to e-business growth. Internet purists may rail against such procedures, but they exist for perfectly good reasons.

Consider the situation from the perspective of a financial executive in an organization. Whether that person is an accountant or has another type of background, he or she is familiar with the concept of internal controls. These are procedures — often referred to as checks and balances — that have been put in place to ensure that the company's assets are protected and that all financial transactions are duly recorded. These policies and procedures have long been part of the world of business, and they have an important purpose.

A good example of an internal control is the need to have two signatures on company cheques over a certain dollar value. This ensures that no one person can abscond with corporate funds, because larger payments are always double-checked. The procedure slows things down because of the inevitable scheduling problems that arise when trying to coordinate the activities of two people. Is this a bad thing in the era of Internet time? We think not — it is a procedure that, while it may slow things down, simply makes prudent business sense.

Another good example of an internal control is ensuring that all invoices received are matched up against an original purchase order and a receiving document. Why is this important? The company can make sure that it is paying only for goods that have been properly authorized for purchase and have actually been delivered. By matching up invoices to the other documents, a company protects itself against paying for things that it has not ordered or received.

Along comes e-biz, with new procedures and methods of generating purchase orders, recording receipt of products, and receiving invoices. People involved in promoting e-commerce — the ones who buy into the rushed mentality of Internet time — suddenly run up against the need for smoothly functioning internal controls. "But we need to go on Internet time," they cry. "We need to move quickly — this is a fast economy! We've got to be able to speed up, process information faster, and get with it!"

They want to go quickly, but, as the saying goes, haste makes waste. A company need not throw out perfectly good internal controls simply so it can charge ahead in a hurry. Checks and balances do slow things down, but they are an important part of the process by which a company manages and protects itself.

MYTH #7: "X" IS THE NEXT BIG THING
REALITY: THERE IS NO NEXT BIG THING

The wreckage of the dot-com age is littered with the visions of those who believed they had come up with something revolutionary. They had found the "next big thing."

There have been many "next big things" over the past few years. The phrase "big thing" has become part of our lexicon, and entire books have been written on the topic. But consider some of the big things you may have heard about. We have put together a quick laundry list of just a few initiatives that were touted as being the next big thing:

- **Network computers.** Back in the early days of the Internet (1996), Larry Ellison of Oracle Corp. loudly proclaimed his belief that the PC was dead, and that we would soon be able to access the Internet via an extremely low-cost "network computer." Such computers would be devoid of hard disks, might cost as little as a hundred dollars, and would bring the Internet to the masses.

There was great excitement and massive hype about the concept — this would cause use of the Internet to explode. But the NC, as it came to be known, never really arrived. Those that eventually appeared were expensive, clunky, and sometimes slow — so much so that people ignored them and continued buying PCs. There have been a number of notable attempts to develop Internet-only computing devices, but few of them have been successful. Most of the world continues to access the Internet through their PCs.

- **Push technology.** Remember Pointcast? It was an application that emerged in the mid-nineties and acted like a screen saver on your computer, sending you a steady stream of up-to-date news, stock quotes, weather forecasts, and other information. It was greeted by a deluge of media coverage about how Internet users could sit at their computers and be on the receiving end of a flood of customized information. Rather than having to pull information off the Internet, they would have it "pushed" out to them.

  Venture capital streamed towards anything that had the word "push" in its executive summary, and a flood of new software sloshed into the marketplace. Push was the future of the Internet! Microsoft jumped on the bandwagon, filling Windows 98 with push technologies that cluttered up the desktop so much that people didn't know what they were doing anymore. Of course, people were soon drowning in information, and doing everything they could to uninstall all the push-related software. Frankly, push was a pain in the neck.

- **M-commerce.** The bust in online shopping came right around the time that Internet-based mobile phone technology was appearing on the scene, in the late 1990s. Those who weren't busy rushing to become B2B marketplaces were setting themselves up for "m-commerce," or mobile commerce. Part of the drive behind this enthusiasm was the rapid pace at which the Japanese seemed to be adopting wireless Internet services. People in the Internet and telecom industries convinced themselves that the next big Internet revenue source would be m-commerce — shopping on the wireless Internet. They seem to have jumped to the conclusion that even though people didn't want to shop on the Internet, surely they would want to do so through their cellphones.

It was one of the most bizarre stretches of logic we have ever seen. Don't get us wrong — we believe that there is a big emerging market in the wireless Internet, as witnessed by the massive success of devices such as the Blackberry e-mail pager from RIM. But the idea of doing transactions on a cellphone begs incredulity. At one point, we ourselves were equipped by a public relations company with a new "Internet cellphone." We discovered that we could use it to buy a book through Amazon.com, a fact that the wireless Internet industry was positively gushing about. We thought it was one of the dumbest ideas we had ever come across. What would ever possess us to buy a book on the Internet through a cellphone? It just seemed to us like a really silly idea.

- **"Free" PCs with free Internet access.** As Internet mania was beginning to explode, some entrepreneurs thought of a novel concept: Provide people with free PCs and free Internet access. Give it all away in order to capture eyeballs, and you'll build a market. It was the next big thing — business based on giving stuff away. Free services sprouted instantly, like mushrooms after a rainstorm, hoping to gather enough visitors to be able to charge a hefty advertising fee.

  People quickly became annoyed by the intrusive advertisements and constant interruptions on their freebies. Online discussion groups were flooded with instructions on how to disable the advertising on the free PCs. Many advertisers didn't even bother to sign on, realizing that the market they could reach was less than exciting. Why? People who signed up often didn't have a demographic profile that interested them, or worse, provided false information about themselves.

- **Portals.** Ah, portals. What a period of hype began with the invention of this word! Suddenly every owner of a search engine, Web directory, or news site rushed to transform it into an online portal. Portals were the future. They were the business model that would validate the Internet! They would be everything to everyone: People would adopt favourite portals and stand by them loyally.

  What was a portal? A place that featured everything you needed on the Internet, all in one site. A directory, search engine, free e-mail, calendaring and scheduling, chat groups, travel booking, online video — you name it, they would cram it in there. Suddenly everyone wanted to run a portal, because once again they believed that massive new revenues would result from all those captured eyeballs. So many people would hang out in portals that advertising revenue would flow like the waters of the Amazon.

Right. Have you noticed that no one seems to be talking much about portals these days?

- **Virtual currency.** Once the idea of Internet commerce and online shopping began to have credence, there was no shortage of visionaries and dot-com start-ups intent on creating new ways of paying for the goods. They weren't just going to come up with new transaction methods, they were going to devise entirely new currencies! Companies such as Cybercash, Digicash, and others planned to set up their own forms of online currency and establish their own unique payment systems. People behind these initiatives spoke of a future in which, almost overnight, they would render irrelevant the supremacy of the U.S. dollar in the global economy.

  Well, it didn't happen quite that way. Surveys continue to show that most online payments are made with traditional credit cards — MasterCard, VISA, and American Express. The concept of new, virtual currencies has all but disappeared.

- **Interactive television.** This particular next big thing is like a nightmare that won't go away. Every once in a while it rears its ugly head, being promoted by television executives who somehow think that people will want to surf the Internet through their TVs.

  We ridiculed the idea of interactive TV in 1994 in our first book, we ridiculed it again when WebTV first appeared on the scene, and it seems that we will have to ridicule it well into the future, as it continues to be floated as the "next big thing." It's like a whack-a-mole game, trying to slam down this dumb idea every time it appears.

  Why is it dumb? For the simple reason that people like to vegetate in front of their TVs — to echo the words of John Lennon, they want to turn off their minds, relax, and let their minds float downstream. It's beyond us why the heck they would want to interrupt their couch-potato reveries to surf the Web or answer their e-mail.

- **Convergence.** Convergence is a close cousin to interactive television. It too keeps popping up, but it regularly undergoes a complex metamorphosis. Convergence is the secret of success, say the new media executives. Then they decide that content is the secret of success. No, aggregating content is the secret of success. Wait — aggregating content and calling it a portal is the key to success. Sorry, that's not it — creating a portal where multiple methods of interacting converge is the key to success.

Like you, we aren't quite sure what they're talking about either. We favour Marc Andreessen's reaction to interactive television and convergence: "Whenever anyone says 'convergence,' reach for your wallet. . . . The whole concept that people will want to interact with their television set is silly. Interactive television happens when your football team loses, and you pitch a beer can at the screen" ("Act II: What's still true — and what was never true — about the Internet," *Fast Company,* February 1, 2001).

Few "big things" turn out to be that big, for the simple reason that much of the change coming about with the Internet and e-biz is not revolutionary, but incremental.

MYTH #8: "FIRST-TO-MARKET" NEW BUSINESS MODELS ARE KEYS TO BUSINESS SUCCESS
REALITY: THERE IS NO ONE DEFINITIVE BUSINESS MODEL

"Next big thing" thinking over the years has given us a steady progression of "definitive" business models. Once people came to believe that they had a definitive model, they thought they could exploit it to become the winner in a particular category on the Internet. Be the first to establish an online school-textbook site? You'd own the category. Be the first to sell pet food? A slam dunk towards owning online pet food sales. It was called "first-mover advantage" or "first to market," and it dominated the spin of e-biz for quite some time.

It wasn't until the dot-com collapse that people realized this too was a fallacy. The problem was that the basic business models behind first-to-market thinking were flawed. It's easy to dream up a new Internet-based business model. It's another thing altogether to make that business model work, and an even greater challenge to rise above the many competitors who have managed to dream up exactly the same business model! After all, there is nothing particularly unique about many of the things you might do on the Internet.

For a time, during the height of dot-com hype, we regularly received calls asking for our advice and involvement in what we came to call the "brilliant idea of the week." Countless entrepreneurs and executives dreamed up what they pitched to us as unique ideas that would make millions. They had discovered the secret, they said. They had found the magic formula.

We would listen patiently and then explain that quite a few people had already had the same idea, and that some existing Web sites already seemed to be quite far down that path. But that didn't matter to many of these instant business pioneers. To those who were drinking the Internet wine, the new business models often seemed so easy — designed to guarantee riches right from the start. In fact, it was hype about the magic of Internet business that led to the dot-com bubble — there were instant profits to be made there!

One business model involved direct sale to consumers of products in a particular category. We saw plenty of specialized sites that focused on selling golf balls, or skis, or wine, for example. This "perfect business model" implied that you could carve out a niche as *the* specialist in a particular category. Given your specialization, it would be easy to make a killing.

A good example of a company adapting to the Internet is Virtual Vineyards, a small Sonoma, Calif., winery that decided to start selling wine on the Internet. Does the idea sound crazy? How does more than $100,000 a month profit sound? After being on the Internet for just over six months, Virtual Vineyards had hit the jackpot. You can bet they never will regret advertising on the Internet.

"TOP 10 EXCUSES FOR IGNORING THE INTERNET," *USA TODAY*, JANUARY 1, 1997

A hundred thousand dollars a month in profit? Hardly. VirtualVineyards has since become Wine.com, just one more struggling dot-com. The idea that you can be an Internet category-killer has been pretty well disproved.

Wine.com has laid off 75 employees, nearly 25 percent of the Napa online retailer's payroll.

Co-founder Peter Granoff said the reduction to 235 from 310 employees "is not part of dot-com cratering" but rather the result of getting rid of overlapping staff. . . . Granoff declined to provide specific sales figures on Wine.com, which is privately owned, or to comment on rumors that the company might be running short of capital.

"WINE.COM FIRES 75 AFTER MERGER WITH WINESHOPPER.COM,"
SAN FRANCISCO CHRONICLE, JANUARY 11, 2001

What was the problem? Suggesting that a single business model can guarantee success trivializes the nature of business. Literally thousands of industries follow certain business models, and there are hundreds of thousands of variations of the models within the subcomponents of those industries. To suggest that it is possible to devise one "killer" or definitive business model — one that will apply to every industry in every sector — is just plain silly.

Along with the concept of the killer business model came the belief that certain business concepts were fundamental to success on the Internet, these among them:

- First-to-market will always win.
- Brands get built overnight.
- Aggressive growth at all costs is the key to market dominance.

The collapse of the dot-com sector clearly showed the fallacy of such thinking. Business is complex, and every business is different. Different markets are massively complex. The Internet is a technology that will transform many industries and markets, but in vastly different ways, and over time, not overnight. The idea that one can dream up an instant, cookie-cutter business model and apply it to a whole bunch of different industries is indicative of the type of perilous thinking that drove many dot-coms to their deaths.

MYTH #9: YOU'LL BE OUT OF BUSINESS IF YOU DON'T USE THE INTERNET
REALITY: YOU'LL BE OUT OF BUSINESS IF YOU GO ONLINE WITHOUT A GOOD REASON

If you're not on the Internet by 2000, you'll be out of business.

PATRICIA SEYBOLD, INTERNATIONALLY
RENOWNED TECHNOLOGY GURU

Made in 1994, this statement was widely repeated, and quickly became one of the mantras of business on the Internet. Many similar observations and comments were also made, on a fairly wide-ranging basis. For example, plenty of people told existing retailers that those dot-com upstarts would put them out of business, which is why they had better get involved in a hurry.

In 10 years, as momentum picks up, the amount of sales in stores will decline. Many physical stores will go from making money to losing money. They're going to have to restructure tremendously or even shut down.

FULTON MACDONALD (RETAIL CONSULTANT WITH INTERNATIONAL
BUSINESS DEVELOPMENT), "PERSONAL TECHNOLOGY: SHOPPING ONLINE —
YOUR NEXT PURCHASE IS JUST A CLICK AWAY," *SEATTLE TIMES*, SEPTEMBER 22, 1996

There are still a few more years to go before it's 2006, but based on the results so far, we think that this suggestion will prove to be wrong.

Along with the increase in such comments has come a regular stream of buzz-phrases from government and business groups and the high-tech sector, all eager to spur along efforts to embrace e-biz. This mantra states that businesses are falling behind in the e-commerce area, and that we had better catch up if we are to survive in the newly emerging global wired economy.

It's Okay Not to Use the Internet

We don't want to disparage such efforts — we do believe in e-biz and think that executives need a lot of encouragement to adapt to the changing world of business. But let's be honest about what is happening here.

It's okay if you choose not to sell on the Internet. Take fashion retailer Holt Renfrew's decision in 2000 to stop selling on the Internet. Some people interpreted that to mean that e-commerce has been a flop, and others were quick to peg them as "not with the times." That's not the case at all. There's simply no point in doing something on the Internet if you can't make money at it.

Extreme statements like "If you aren't on the Internet, you won't survive" do little to help people adapt to the realities of e-biz. Many businesspeople, such as the marina operator we met in Chapter 1, have seen little real evidence that companies are disappearing because they didn't embrace the Internet. Indeed, the only casualties appear to be a lot of Internet and dot-com companies! Obviously, the idea that you will quickly go out of business if you don't adapt to the Internet is one of the sillier myths that came out of the early Internet age, and we don't need to say much more about it.

But what is the reality? Companies will discover that, over time, there will be increasing demands by suppliers and customers for them to become participants in the network. There is no doubt that transactions of the global economy are moving slowly and steadily to the

Internet. New, Internet-based competitors will challenge existing businesses and displace their profit margins. Every company is going to have to work hard to figure out how to deal with the challenges.

But companies can choose to operate in the global economy without participating in the Internet, and probably will be fine for quite some time. They should, however, be aware of the ever-increasing negative implications of such a decision. They will, for example, be unable to respond to massive price competition from new competitors, to reach new markets that the competitors can, or to streamline cost structures through the efficiencies that can come from adoption of the Internet for transaction purposes.

But it's silly to suggest that they'll be out of business in a short time if they don't instantly throw themselves heart and soul into the Internet. And to suggest that you get involved by throwing strategic common-sense out the window is wrong as well. Every e-commerce or e-business initiative needs a good business case behind it. We do believe that businesses should get involved with the Internet somehow, but in a way that makes sense for them and for their industries at that time.

MYTH #10: THE INTERNET HAS NO RULES
REALITY: OLD-ECONOMY RULES STILL APPLY

The biggest myth of all is that it is possible to build a business in which profit doesn't matter and the rules for running an old-economy company don't apply. With it came promotion of the concept that many "old-fashioned" business ideas and methods simply weren't necessary, particularly when it came to profits.

We are a retailer without the financial burden of in-store inventory or actual stores.

GLENDA M. DORCHAK (FORMER PRESIDENT AND COO, VALUE AMERICA),
QUOTED IN "THE SLOWEST MODEM IS FASTER THAN THE SHORTEST DRIVE,"
RICHMOND TIMES-DISPATCH, NOVEMBER 9, 1998

The likelihood of a traditional brick and mortar retailer succeeding in this space we think is extremely remote.

CRAIG WINN (FOUNDER AND CHAIRMAN OF VALUE AMERICA),
IN "VALUE AMERICA FOUNDER," CNNFN *CAPITAL IDEAS*, MAY 11, 1999

Oops — we just checked, and Value America is no longer around.

The "New Math" Doesn't Really Work

One of the authors wrote about the foolishness of the dot-com financial model in his weekly *Globe and Mail* column back in 1999, just as the dot-com period was starting to peak. The article was written to put into perspective many of the silly financial assumptions of some dot-com entrepreneurs and venture capitalists. Apparently instantly, they had come up with new methods of analyzing and valuing companies (perhaps as a way of justifying their activities). The author noted just how ridiculous things had become by commenting on these interesting financial methodologies:

Revenue or sales. For dot-com companies, this is a widely unused and unnecessary financial number. Ideally, if such a financial measure yields a number, it should be as close to zero as possible.

EPS. In the old economy, this means earnings per share. A meaningless statistic for dot-com companies, given the distinct lack of earnings. However, the meaning of EPS can be slightly altered to become an important measure to judge the potential success of a dot-com company. Closely examine the EPSM, or earnings-per-square-metre ratio. If this number is above 2, it indicates that the company employs few people over the age of 30, which will help ensure that the company isn't contaminated by any old economy ideas.

Assets. You've got to be kidding. Dot-com companies don't believe in such an archaic concept. The only assets might be a few computers, and a fridge stuffed full of Twinkies and Jolt Cola.

A better measure is the PRAISE ratio (which stands for PR agencies with Internet startup expertise). If this number is high, it means that the company has hired the best agencies to help build hype about the company's potential.

SE. Old-economy companies refer to it as shareholder equity. Dot-coms refer to it as "suckers equity."

JIM CARROLL, "DOT-COMS HAVE THEIR OWN MATH," OCTOBER 21, 1999

Reaction to the article was interesting — the author took a fair amount of abuse from dot-com mavens, who wrote to him that he just didn't get it. Well, he did get it, as did many others in the financial press and the business community who kept their wits about them as the Internet investment orgy raced to its frantic conclusion. Today? No longer hailed as heroes, dot-com millionaires and venture capitalists are now being denounced as villains, and unhappy investors are casting about trying to find someone to blame (other than the obvious persons — themselves).

We are now seeing a flood of articles reminding people that, at the end of the day, old-economy rules matter most.

The Internet economy was going to change all the rules. But the past 12 months have forced investors to reconsider, with the volatile stock market providing ample reminders that the fundamentals of business and investing remain the same. The medium may be different, but investment professionals say the most important lesson of 2000 is that the "new economy" is really not so different from the old.

"NEW-ECONOMY EUPHORIA, OLD INVESTING LESSON,"
AUSTIN AMERICAN-STATESMAN, DECEMBER 31, 2000

Enough said.

STICK TO REALITY

If you read this chapter in a negative frame of mind, you might be convinced that the entire Internet and e-biz concept has been a giant fraud. While much of what has been said about it certainly has been fraudulent, one simple fact remains: There are plenty of reasons why the Internet will be adopted throughout the world as a way of doing business. Good Internet-based business models exist, and the Internet does offer cost-saving opportunities, proven marketing methods, public relations value, and countless other business benefits.

But if you get caught up in the hype and the myths, then you start to do the wrong things. As *PC Week* said back in 1994, "The Internet frenzy is causing otherwise smart companies to make reckless decisions" ("Why 1995 Is the Year of Living Dangerously," January 28, 1994).

We are perhaps two of the biggest believers in the potential of the Internet and e-biz. We will, however, admit something. We were actually quite thrilled by the collapse of the dot-com sector and the ridiculous overvaluation of Internet companies on the stock market. That crash helped bring some sanity back to the proceedings.

In the next chapter, we will walk you through why we believe that the Internet and e-biz are still significant, which will help you realize that there are still plenty of business and career opportunities to be found in e-biz.

Chapter 3

Why E-biz Still Matters

The technology market entered 2000 to the sound of champagne corks popping. It exited to the sound of a bugle playing Taps. "They've thrown out the baby and the bath water, the towels, the soap, the shampoo and stopper, and they are burning everything in the bathroom and are going to start on the rest of the house," says Cristina Morgan, co-director of investment banking at J. P. Morgan Chase. "After they burn everything down, they will rebuild it. It always comes back."

"TECH YEAR BEGINS WITH FIZZ OF CHAMPAGNE, ENDS WITH SOUND OF BUGLE PLAYING TAPS," *INVESTMENT DEALERS DIGEST*, JANUARY 8, 2001

IF YOU WANT TO BE PART OF THE WORLD OF E-BIZ, YOU'VE GOT TO GET beyond the skeptics, including those who wallow in dot-com gloom, and think in the long term. Sure, there's been a temporary hiccup on the voyage, but our long-term perspective is that the Internet, as a system, has barely scratched the surface in terms of its impact on our daily lives and on the way that business is conducted. We think — and we have been saying this consistently over the years — that it will take five, ten, twenty, or even more years before the true impact of the Internet is felt. While the past six years have been an incredible ride, we believe that there is still much more to come. Indeed, the trip has barely even started.

To appreciate this fact is to appreciate what we believe are the four fundamental drivers that will continue to move the Internet and e-commerce forward, well into the future.

THE INTERNET IS PART OF PEOPLE'S LIVES
It's kind of funny when you think about the recent overreaction to problems around the Internet. If you listen to the media, as we pointed out

in Chapter 1, it would seem that people are abandoning the Internet in droves. Remember the "news story" we described, that claimed millions were shutting down their computers and moving on? It is more than an understatement to suggest that was an overreaction.

Don't get us wrong. Based on our own experiences, we don't doubt that some people have tired of certain aspects of the Internet. Some activities that it was thought people might do online (for example, shopping or watching TV) have not turned out to be major phenomena. Also, there is usually an initial period of overuse because of users' fascination with the novelty, but then most people scale back this kind of online excess over time.

But, having said that, we truly believe that the fundamental driving factor behind the Internet, and one that makes every concept in this book valid in the long term, is a simple fact.

People are using the Internet, will continue to use the Internet, and will use it for an ever-increasing number of day-to-day activities, both personal and work-related. Look around you, and you can see the signs of how the Internet has come to influence our behaviour and become part of our daily routine. Sit back and think about the people you know and how they are using the Internet. You'll quickly understand that it has become an integral part of our lives.

Our favourite story in this vein involves a neighbour of one of the authors.

The Weather Junkie

The author's neighbour is a landscape architect, a smart guy who has built up a successful business, but who certainly isn't much of a computer wizard. He uses his PC only to play a few family games, put together customer quotes, and write letters — and for one other very important purpose: to check the weather. After all, the weather is probably one of the most important factors affecting what he does on a day-to-day basis.

It is fascinating to realize how important a role the Internet has taken on for this guy. When he gets up in the morning, the first thing that he does — before he has a shower, eats breakfast, or does anything else — is check the weather on the Internet. Why? Because the forecast will help him determine what he will do that day, how he will schedule his crews, which activities he will work on, and what supplies he will order.

Sure, he could access a weather report from the newspaper, radio, or television. But those reports are usually rather general and cover a wide area. On the Internet, he can check the weather radar, view the rotation and direction of approaching systems, and get his own sense of how conditions will affect the areas where his clients live, and thus where he should work that day. The level of detail he can access is stunning, compared to the alternatives. The Internet has helped him to become his own specialized weather forecaster. In other words, the Internet has become fundamental to the way that he manages and schedules his business.

The Internet is a fad? Well, not to this fellow — you should see what happens when his cable modem connection goes down; it can get rather ugly. His routine is interrupted and his ability to forecast potentially poor conditions goes to pieces because he can't get the precise weather information he is used to, and hence can't do as good a job at scheduling his crews.

The man is an online weather junkie. He's addicted, and he won't be abandoning the Internet any time soon. The Internet is weaving itself into other aspects of his life, too. He finds himself going online for a growing number of activities, such as accessing news, financial information, and other material of relevance to what he does on a day-to-day basis.

This situation is a microcosm of what is happening around the world. Regardless of the circumstances, the person, or the company, the Internet is weaving itself into the daily lives of hundreds of millions of people worldwide. Everyone is finding reasons to sign on, use the Internet, and keep going back to it. And, over time, they find that it

---

PEOPLE HAVE COME TO USE THE INTERNET IN THE AREA OF HEALTH CARE IN VERY SIGNIFICANT NUMBERS.

- In the first quarter of 2000, 40.9 million adults were using the Internet to research health care.
- Fifty-four percent were using the Internet to look up additional information after seeing a pharmaceutical advertisement.
- Seventy-two percent indicated that they rely on the Internet to learn more about health-care products, compared to 43 percent who ask their doctor and 17 percent who call the pharmaceutical company 800 number.

Source: "Internet Customer Service: Is your pharmaceutical call center prepared?"
Telemarketing & Call Center Solutions, October 1, 2000

comes to play an increasing role in what they do day by day, whether they are interested in financial information, health care, or any other topic. This means that tremendous opportunities with the Internet and electronic commerce will continue to exist, well into the future.

Purchasing Behaviour

As the Internet weaves its way into the daily lives of people like the weather junkie, it comes to have a huge impact on their day-to-day behaviour. This behaviour includes spending.

While there is now no doubt that online shopping has been a bust in many sectors of the economy, the Internet nonetheless influences the shopping that people do in the "real world." As an information utility, the Internet has come to play a huge role in our behaviour as consumers and purchasers. When someone is thinking of buying something, either for their own use or on behalf of a company they work for, increasingly they will turn to the Internet.

One of our favourite things to do when speaking at a conference is to ask the crowd how many people have recently purchased a vehicle on the Internet. Quite predictably, few hands, if any, go up. Then we ask if anyone has recently *researched* a new car or vehicle on the Internet before going to a dealership. Almost every hand is raised — a good demonstration of the role and power of the Internet.

Another favourite example is asking who in the crowd has bought a new home in the past three years. We then ask those with raised hands to keep their hands raised if they used the Internet to look up mortgage rates and other information related to their purchase. Almost every hand stays up.

What do these examples suggest? Potential buyers venturing into an automobile dealership have quite a different approach from five years ago. They are far readier to challenge, more aware of their alternatives and variations in prices, and more in tune with margins and cost-saving opportunities. The dealers who are negotiating with them are in a considerably less comfortable and secure position than they were previously. And this shift means that both automobile companies and dealers must be prepared to use the Internet as one of the methods through which they deal with customers.

In the financial world, use of the Internet has caused a subtle but distinct shift in power — away from the provider of the mortgage and over to the consumer, who is now far more aware of the alternatives. That small shift in power will have big repercussions, because it means that organizations will have to work harder, utilizing the Internet as one of their marketing tools, in order to attract or keep the business of that customer.

Overall, it means that a gradual power shift is happening in the world of business, in which the consumer is far more empowered than ever before. In this new, wired world, customers will demand to know the full range of products and services offered by an organization — in electronic form, via the Web — even though they may prefer to do business with that company in the "real world." The implication that flows from this shift is that, far from disappearing, the Web sites of every organization, large and small, will come to play an ever-increasing role in the way that companies market to their customer base. They will need to make the Internet a central part of their customer-service equation.

The Electronic Customer/Business Relationship

Not only has the Internet come to influence the way that people make their purchasing decisions, it has altered their expectations of how they should be able to deal with a company in terms of service and support. Not only do they expect to be able to access product information that might help them with purchasing decisions, they expect fast, extremely high-quality support through the Web. They expect to be able to fire off an e-mail question to any organization and receive an almost instantaneous response.

A fascinating thing about this expectation is that it presents every company with a conundrum: People have come to expect every company they deal with to offer the same quality of service that they get from the most stellar sites. After people experience amazing support through a Web site such as Dell Computers (an organization considered to be one of the leaders in effective online support), they expect a similar quality of experience with every organization that they deal with online. Hence, the field of customer service is becoming one of the most important areas of business today, and will continue to do so well into the future. The spending that will occur in this field over the next five to ten years, as customers increasingly demand an electronic relationship, will make earlier levels of corporate investment in Internet initiatives pale by comparison.

In order to attract and retain business, companies will have no choice but to become experts at online customer support. But doing that is not easy — a lot of effort will be required. Spending on online customer support will evolve to become a major part of overall corporate expenditures. This is such an important issue that we devote the following chapter to the issue of customer support in the wired economy.

ELECTRONIC BUSINESS CAN SAVE COMPANIES MONEY

Another bottom-line issue driving the implementation of the Internet and e-commerce within the corporate sector is this fact: *The Internet fulfills many important business needs, one of the most significant of which is that it helps companies save money.*

Quite simply, there are many opportunities for organizations to shave costs by changing the way they conduct business. Our paper-based economy is tremendously inefficient, and many an organization has clearly demonstrated that moving over to electronic transaction systems can save significant sums of money. Thus, one of the major areas of effort with the Internet during the next decade is going to be projects that involve a slow, steady move away from paper-based transaction systems to electronic ones.

This change will be such a big component of e-biz because of the scope and complexity of the effort. While the cost savings are there, they are tough to realize. As discussed in the previous chapter, it takes a lot of hard work, effort, and senior management commitment to truly "do e-business." We believe that the spending in this area has only just begun, because companies have only recently begun to figure out the nature of the opportunity. Only now are sophisticated large-scale projects that focus on Internet-based re-engineering commencing. Why? It appears from our perspective that, just as the dot-com collapse was beginning, senior executives in companies large and small finally figured out the real strategic purpose of the Internet.

Yes, they had been confused for quite some time before this realization set in. For a while, for example, it seemed that the best opportunity was in online shopping. Then it was new business models, such as buyer-driven pricing and online auctions, and the establishment of entirely new lines of business. This was followed by the hype around B2B, much of which concentrated on industry e-marketplaces. Yet, just as these buzz-phrase opportunities were proving to be a bust in many sectors, a more focused, rational perspective was taking hold. Executives came to realize one simple, important, undeniable fact: At the most fundamental level, *the Internet offers organizations the opportunity to save money.*

The fact that businesses have finally come to realize this is the driving factor behind many significant corporate initiatives to be found on the Internet today and in the future. During the pathetic spectacle of ongoing dot-com shutdowns, real companies with real businesses have been busy developing and implementing significant e-biz strategies focused on the goal of saving money.

We described this critical aspect of e-business in our book *Lightbulbs to Yottabits: How to Profit by Understanding the Internet of the Future*, thus:

> . . . *the smart businesses involved with the Internet have come to realize that the real benefit of e-commerce isn't necessarily found in selling online, but instead, comes from changing the way that current business is conducted.*
>
> *They know that the question isn't, "How do I use the Internet to make money?" but rather, "How do I use the Internet to save money?"*
>
> . . . *We think that through the next five years most businesses will have to realize that the real potential and the biggest returns with e-commerce won't be from the sale of products to consumers. They will have come to realize that it comes from using it as a tool to save money, through the re-engineering of their business processes with their customers, suppliers, trading partners, and others with whom they have a business relationship.*
>
> JIM CARROLL AND RICK BROADHEAD, *LIGHTBULBS TO YOTTABITS:*
> *HOW TO PROFIT BY UNDERSTANDING THE INTERNET OF THE FUTURE* (1999)

Expanding Online Systems Outward

Until the arrival of the Internet, the business world had barely begun to extend its transaction systems to outside companies. Suddenly they were preparing to do so in an online world.

The easiest way to understand the potential of Internet cost savings is to consider electronic billing. It is a method by which hydro and telephone companies, department stores, and other organizations can allow customers to access their bills electronically via a Web site and pay for those bills online, rather than having to deal with a paper statement. It is an important opportunity for such organizations, and many are actively pursuing e-billing operations. An Angus Reid survey near the end of 2000 indicated that 87 percent of Canada's top billers were actively looking at technology that would let them deliver invoices and receive payment electronically. They all plan to stop delivering paper statements to customers who choose electronic billing.

What's driving them to do this? Cost savings. Most estimates suggest that an electronic bill will cost only a fraction of a paper bill. That's why you will soon see organizations such as utilities, department stores, and even governments offering the option of paying your bills online. To do so, you'll visit a secure mailbox, read your electronic bill, and press a few keys to transfer money from your bank account to the company. (We'll focus more on this opportunity in Chapter 4.)

E-biz applications need not be complex in order to achieve cost savings. Many can take advantage of what might be considered the "low-hanging fruit" — Internet cost-saving applications that are so easy to develop, and offer such a level of cost savings, that they are a natural to implement. Of course, there are also far more sophisticated initiatives, which we describe later in this book. Not surprisingly, high-tech firms have led the way; for example, Microsoft has transformed its purchasing process through the Internet.

Expanded online systems will help make cost savings one of the most massive areas of opportunity with the Internet, through what we call "extended enterprise transaction systems." As we state in the next chapter, though, it can take a while to realize those cost savings, and that factor will provide many new career opportunities.

OUTSOURCING IS CHANGING THE NATURE OF THE ORGANIZATION

Another reason why the Internet will continue to have a major effect on business well into the future is that it is leading to a subtle shift in the very nature of the organization. We are moving towards what we might call the "outsourced economy" — one in which there will be tremendous opportunities for specialized organizations with particular types of expertise. An outsourced economy is one in which an increasing number of companies will decide to get rid of "non-core" functions in order to concentrate on their main mission and goals. This model will lead to many new career and business opportunities.

Outsourcing is nothing new; it has been a key component of our global economy for quite some time. During the past few decades, we have seen many companies assign responsibility for certain core functions to third parties, such as automakers outsourcing the manufacturing of particular car parts. In addition, various corporate services and activities have long been outsourced. For example, major companies have been outsourcing computer and information technology services for quite some time.

We believe that the connectivity afforded by the Internet will accelerate the pace of outsourcing, for two reasons. First, the emergence of sophisticated supply-chain systems allows a greater degree of interaction between business partners. Second, the connectivity of the Internet allows a company to outsource entire business functions and departments, because the information processed by those departments can now be accessed from anywhere.

Supply-Chain Management

As we explain in Chapter 4, we are on the tip of the iceberg when it comes to the use of e-biz technology within the corporate sector. While companies have come to understand that e-biz offers cost savings, some are also realizing that they have been thinking about those savings in very narrow terms, focusing strictly on interaction with customers.

There is much greater potential than that, which is why the concept of "supply-chain management" has become an important issue within the business community. Supply-chain management involves using e-biz to streamline the way companies with vested interests can function together, by managing the transactions and interactions that occur between those companies. A number of companies — from the supplier of raw materials through to the organization that assembles them into a finished product — might work together on a coordinated basis to streamline their business transactions and interactions so that they take place through the Internet.

Supply-chain management will lead to greater outsourcing; it brings to an industry an efficiency in communications that allows companies to rely to a greater degree upon their partners. We'll take a deeper look at this issue in Chapter 4.

Business Process Outsourcing

We believe that another significant trend that will play out during the next five to twenty years will see companies outsourcing entire functional departments. It used to be that companies outsourced only certain activities, such as information technology. But other departments are now set to go, fuelled by the connectivity afforded by the Internet.

Why? Because, with the Internet, a company can now access via a Web browser any information being maintained by a third-party organization. The result is that, if they outsource, say, their accounts payable department to a third-party organization, they can have instant access to their accounts payable information at any time. No longer do they have to wait for the outsourcer to send paper reports or other details. They can access any needed transaction details, reports, or other information, directly and without complication.

While outsourcing has been with us for some time, inefficiency in communications has held many such initiatives back. With the Internet, that inefficiency disappears. This means that people who work in certain areas — such as receivables, payables, fixed-asset management, or claims processing — may find themselves working for a different employer at some point in the future. Yet they'll be doing exactly the same things as for their present employer, who will have sent the entire department to another company that will do the work for it.

THE PAYROLL EXAMPLE

Companies are waking up to the potential of outsourcing. Consider Ceridian Canada (www.ceridian.ca), a company born in 1998 from combining the payroll services of the TD Bank and CIBC. With a dedicated staff of 1,300 people, they now process payroll for almost 17 percent of the Canadian workforce — about 2.4 million Canadians rely upon the company to process some 58 million paycheques per year. In effect, a significant number of Canadian companies have decided that they don't want to have to worry about the payroll function; they are willing to pay an organization like Ceridian to do it on their behalf.

Outsourcing has proven itself in the financial area, with payroll. With the increasing role of the Internet, we are going to see a lot of specialist companies decide they can do the same thing with other activities.

The Emergence of Business Service Providers

Helping to drive the trend towards outsourcing is the emergence of organizations that allow a company to utilize (or "rent") sophisticated financial and other software systems without having to buy and implement the systems directly.

In the hype days of the dot-com period, we saw the emergence of a lot of "application service providers." These organizations promised you exactly that capability. Unfortunately, many of them crashed and burned because of lack of take-up by companies and also some challenges with their business model. Interestingly, however, some people are still promoting this concept, and they are evolving into what are known as "business service providers."

The business model has changed a bit, though, in that not only will these companies "rent" the software to you, they will also take over your entire financial function. Take a look at Finetrics (www.finetrics.com) as an example. They'll rent you a sophisticated financial application, but they have also done a deal with Arthur Andersen, who will send in specialists to do all the day-to-day accounting you might need. Another example is Ledgent (www.ledgent.com), an organization that specializes in taking on outsourced accounting functions.

Are companies subscribing to the idea of outsourcing entire departments? By all means — a few years ago, GM signed a ten-year, $250 million (U.S.) deal that had Arthur Andersen take over its accounts receivable and other financial functions. There are some big dollars driving this trend.

The emergence of this entirely new aspect of the outsourcing industry might cause havoc for anyone whose career involves the pushing of paper. Estimates from the publication *Digital Systems Report* (www.computereconomicsstore.com) in its Spring 2000 issue indicate that half the organizations with sophisticated financial systems will be turning these functions over to third parties. Why is this happening? Because companies are realizing that the connectivity of the wired economy allows them to dispense with routine functions. They can focus on what needs to be done in terms of strategy, sales, and other key activities that improve the bottom line. Everything else is just procedures that can be done by someone else. So, they get rid of them. This fits perfectly with the "core competencies" theme that has swirled through the business world for the past several years.

If you put together all of these trends, you will realize that what we said about the nature of the organization changing rings true. An organization today consists of a group of people who perform a wide variety of functions, all under the corporate umbrella. Tomorrow, an organization will still consist of a group of people who perform a wide variety of functions, but many of them will work for different third-party organizations and business partners.

INTERNET INFRASTRUCTURE WILL GROW AS BUSINESSES ADAPT

If you accept all of the reasoning above, then it is only logical to conclude that investment and growth in the infrastructure of the Internet and e-commerce will continue. Yet the recession of 2001 put a damper on the whole tech sector. For a time, it seemed as if there would be little infrastructure investment, and that the spending seen in the early days of the Internet would slow down.

Once again, our theory is different. We think that, after a temporary lull, infrastructure spending will once again skyrocket, and e-biz and the Internet will continue their relentless march forward. Why? Because we can liken the early days of e-biz to the early days of the Apollo moon program.

The Velcro Theory

From 1962 to 1969, the U.S. experienced an explosion of scientific advancements that resulted from efforts to reach the moon. The list of inventions that came directly out of the space program is stunning. First, there's the usual list — Teflon, Velcro, integrated circuits, miniature computer chips and advanced microprocessors, satellites, solar energy, cordless appliances, robotic hands, UV-blocking sunglasses, insulin pumps, and microwaves — each with their roots in the Apollo program.

But many more spin-offs resulted from this tremendous period of creative energy, especially in the field of medicine. Remotely programmable low-power, one-chip pacemakers, laser angioplasty systems, and the ear-canal infrared thermometer were some of the medical advances. Not to forget CAT scanners and MRI technology — these came out of technology originally developed to enhance pictures of the moon and to examine Apollo castings, rocket motors, and other equipment for defects.

Even the shoes you wear may be traced back to Apollo — many of today's fashion shoes are made by a specialized blow-moulding process developed for the Apollo program. In your automobile, the material used to dampen engine noise comes from the insulation barriers made for spacecraft.

Innovations spawned by the space program didn't occur just in the technical area. NASA made tremendous advances in business methodologies involving program management, supply-chain management, and interactive, inter-organizational design concepts. As the space program wound down, tens of thousands of brilliant engineers, program managers, executives, and other NASA workers would take their new ideas about how processes should work into the business world — ideas about project management, quality control, inter-organization projects, and communication methods, and countless other new business theories. The scope of their efforts was astounding; these people had learned how to manage massively complex undertakings. The Apollo rocket alone had two million working parts, and quality control demanded that not one part could possibly fail.

Here is an extremely important point: The impact of this rapid period of creativity in technology and business methods took a long time to be felt, for all the reasons that we described in the previous chapter. And yet the Apollo program forever changed the world around us, and led to massive ongoing spending on new technologies in a huge number of industries, and major spending in the areas of business theory and management.

So it is with the Internet. There was a remarkable burst of creative energy during the first wave of the Internet, from 1995 to 2000. This energy, fuelled by the dot-coms and technology companies, led to a significant number of new developments in technology, e-commerce, and other software; to new ideas on how business might function; and to fascinating developments in communications technologies. It was an unparalleled period of invention that will, like the Apollo program, take a long time to intertwine itself with the world around us.

The Pace of Change
Significant change takes time, and we think that right now many organizations are simply trying to figure out the massive amount of new technology that is being thrust their way — so many new concepts, so many new ways of doing business, so much potential to change business for the better.

With these new ways of doing business comes a need for new software — the stuff that makes e-biz tick. We certainly can't expect companies to be able to understand and implement this stuff overnight. First, a remarkable learning curve has to be overcome. That's where we have landed in 2001 — and from where the world of business will eventually emerge.

The pace of change and evolution is only going to increase. In January 2000, *Discover* magazine made some fascinating observations about the pace of technological change, commenting that 80 percent of all scientific discoveries in the history of mankind have occurred within the last hundred years. They then went on to note that innovation in the twenty-first century will exceed the twentieth century in the areas of science and technology. This progress will happen not because people are smarter than they were in the past, but simply because connectivity is fuelling a faster exchange of information than ever before. For example, conference papers are posted on the Web almost immediately, reducing delays in the exchange of ideas among scholars and researchers. E-mail allows colleagues in far-flung regions to share their thoughts more quickly than ever before, increasing the pace of development.

Consider the impact of communications in the pharmaceutical and health-care industries. While much medical research must still go through the traditional peer-review process — which helps to ensure its integrity — other information is being shared more rapidly online. The overall result is that the pace of new drug and health-care research has speeded up.

The big difference, almost certainly, is in the transmission of useful information, knowledge and insight. This is happening at a faster and faster pace; and it is becoming less and less costly in the bargain. Faster transmission begets greater discovery.

HARRY C. STONECIPHER, "TECHNOLOGY IN A NETWORKED WORLD,"
EXECUTIVE SPEECHES, AUGUST 1, 2000

So, while the media are reporting with much enthusiasm on the sorry state of e-biz affairs and the slowdown in technology spending, the reality is that the world of technology and e-biz continues to move along. New technologies are continually being invented, computer code is being developed, e-business applications are being built, and new ways of doing business are evolving. We've got a huge and vibrant worldwide high-tech industry: plenty of jobs, massive opportunity, lots of money to be made, and new careers and opportunities continuing to appear in the sector over the long term. We have no doubt that, 20 years out, the growth of Internet infrastructure will be regarded as one of the leading business stories of the early twenty-first century.

CONCLUSION: THE GREED HAS LEFT THE BUILDING

And finally, to our last point. The great dot-com collapse of 2000–2001 was probably the best thing that could have happened to the Internet and e-biz, because it has helped ensure that the strategies behind every Internet initiative will be subject to sound business thinking.

What happened during the past several years with the Internet and e-biz is that basic, primal human greed invaded every aspect of the network and its activities. It led to a situation in which many Internet and e-biz initiatives were limited in their thinking — they were based on the objective of a quick buck. Far too many Internet projects and businesses were designed with the objective of an immediate hit on the stock market, or speedy sale of the new company to venture capitalists or other investors. The goal wasn't to build a real business, but just to get some fast cash — establish a dot-com, get some financing, and watch the dollars flow in!

Sadly, greed overtook simple common sense, which meant that many people who got involved with Internet and e-commerce initiatives — who might otherwise be rational in their thinking — got caught up in the idea that they too could participate in this online nirvana. Of course, the real world doesn't work that way. It takes time, careful thought, and a lot of hard work to build a real, sustainable business. Profits matter, and business fundamentals count. Anyone involved in the implementation of sophisticated technological business systems knows that it takes a lot of effort to deploy those new systems.

Since the dot-com meltdown, the projects and opportunities being pursued and the businesses being built are far more realistic than those of the recent past. The collapse of the bubble has made the reality check of this book possible, so we can help you explore the real business and career opportunities in the Internet economy.

Part II

Business Opportunities

Chapter 4

Electronic Transactions

It may be surprising to some people to realize that even in this new economy with the Internet, close to nine out of ten invoices and payments are still paper-based in the business-to-business sector in the U.S.

DANIEL M. MCGURL (CHAIRMAN AND CEO, BOTTOMLINE TECHNOLOGIES)
ON *WALL STREET CORPORATE REPORTER*, NOVEMBER 13, 2000

FROM OUR PERSPECTIVE, MANY COMPANIES THAT ARE THINKING STRATE-gically about business opportunities of the Internet and e-commerce have been focusing on the wrong question. They've asked themselves how they can use them as a tool to make money. How could they sell or market products? How could they open new markets? How might they use the Internet to establish a new business opportunity?

While those strategies may be important, such a focus has caused companies to miss one area of opportunity that could provide the greatest benefit. It involves asking the question, "How do I use the Internet to save money in the way that I do business?" We touched on this issue in Chapter 3, but we would like to spend some time discussing it in more depth.

The Long Road to the Paperless Office

Our global economy is drowning in paper. But, slowly and inevitably, because of the Internet and e-commerce, it is becoming an electronic economy. Therein lies one of the most important changes that will occur as the business world moves towards e-commerce: Transactions between organizations will increasingly occur electronically. That simple fact is the aspect of the Internet that will result in a lot of new jobs, technologies, companies, and opportunities.

The transition, which is massive in scope and scale, is already well underway. But it won't come about easily. As anyone involved with information technology knows, it takes a tremendous amount of effort to change the way in which an organization processes information. The changeover to a world of electronic inquiry, billing, and payment is one of the most complicated business projects of all time. It will take a huge effort over the next 20 years for companies to wrest themselves away from their addiction to paper. Note that we said "20 years" — we believe that the undertaking is of such massive complexity that it could indeed take that long.

How dare we predict that companies will wean themselves from paper? After all, the corporate sector's track record when it comes to reducing paper usage isn't all that great. People have long said that computers would reduce the use of paper, yet the exact opposite has happened. As we look around, we realize that, far from making paper go away, computers seem to have made things worse.

Promises, Promises

It wasn't supposed to be this way. Back in the 1970s, as computer technology first began to invade the corporate world, it was believed that the economy would soon be based on electronic invoices and cheques. Executives presumed that, because computers could easily process information, they would instantly do away with paper.

In 1975, the head of Xerox Corporation's Research Center in Palo Alto, California, predicted that the use of printed paper would decline dramatically as offices turned to electronic ways of doing business.

As office automation became all the rage in the late seventies and early eighties, the buzz was that we would soon see the "paperless office." Not only would transactions between businesses be paperless, so too would the office environment! We would work, we were told, in an office devoid of paper. Reports abounded of how wonderful it would be — documents and reports would speed along through corporate networks, massive knowledge databases would easily be built, and business would be effortless, since so little time would be needed to bother with paper.

So why is there still so much paper around? The reality of the technological revolution is that computers have a nasty tendency to *increase* the use of paper in the office and corporate environment. One study suggests that we use upwards of two pounds of paper per person per day. Other studies indicate that use of office paper has grown by 30 percent during the last decade. Consider this fact: According to the American Forest and Paper Association, U.S. paper producers shipped almost 30 million tons of paper in 1999, up from 16.1 million tons in 1995. Photocopiers are one of the culprits, admittedly — copier paper usage alone rose by 500,000 tons in just a year, from 1996 to 1997.

> Studies indicate that people spend 15 percent of their working time retrieving documents or other paper, and that 7.5 percent of all paper documents within an office are lost. You can read more about the paperless office at www.cs.mu.oz.au/ ~kwo/paperless.html.

As for electronic cheques and transactions? They seem to be only a pipe dream in many industries. *Wireless* magazine estimates that North Americans write some *63 billion* cheques each year. A third are sent by consumers in payment of their bills, a third are used by companies to pay invoices, and a third are of other types (birthday cheques and such). It is quite clear why so few people are still brave enough to talk about the paperless office!

Business Within a Bubble

Part of the reason the paperless office eludes us is that few companies and industries have managed to link their computer systems with those of their business partners. It is rather bizarre, if you think about it — with all of those computers about, very few transactions between companies actually occur directly from one computer to another. In fact, most of the information that organizations receive from the outside world arrives in paper form, and is then entered — at great expense — into their computer systems. One might think that our economy today is a bit of a game, the objective of which is not to be the last one to send a piece of paper.

> A 1993 study by Lawrence Livermore Labs and Coopers & Lybrand indicated that it costs $250 in staff time to recreate a lost document, and $120 to find a missing document. Simply filing or retrieving a document costs $20.

Think about a typical business transaction. A company wants to purchase a product, so a paper purchase order is sent. When the goods are shipped, a paper shipping document is prepared and a paper invoice is mailed out. The invoice is then paid for with a paper cheque. Of course, if it isn't paid on time, the seller sends out a paper reminder notice indicating that payment is overdue. Once payment is made, the seller sends out a paper statement, indicating that the invoice has been charged and duly paid and including details on any overdue charges that have accrued, for which a separate paper notice might also have been sent!

Why is there still so much exchange of paper within our economy some 40 years after computer technology was first implemented in business? It is because few companies and few industries have figured out how to do business electronically beyond their own walls. The focus of computerization so far has mostly been internal. Organizations simply haven't had time to look at how they might use technology for outside business processes, nor have they the technological foundation on which to build such applications.

This means that, so far, most technological efforts by the corporate sector have been inward looking. They've worked tremendously hard to computerize their operations. They've succeeded in automating much

---

PAPER STATISTICS

- A survey by *Fast Company* asked, "Do you use more paper communication or e-mail in your business?" Eighty-six percent said "more paper."

- According to Hewlett Packard, when e-mail is introduced into an office, printing increases by 40 percent.

- According to CAP Ventures, a Norwell, Massachusetts–based market research firm, the number of pages consumed in U.S. offices has been going up 6 percent each year, and was expected to hit 1.54 trillion by 2000.

- *USA Today*'s "Snapshot of America" column for January 25, 2000, stated that workers print out an average of 32 pages a day from the Internet.

- PriceWaterhouseCoopers' *Technology Forecast* in 1999 stated that 8.8 million sheets of paper are used by a company per $100 million increase in its sales.

- The same *Technology Forecast* stated that 809.3 billion sheets were used by office copiers in 1996 and 1.1 trillion sheets were estimated for 2001, and 787.6 billion sheets were used by laser printers in 1996 and 1.2 trillion were estimated for 2001.

- Alvin Toffler, in *Powershift*, estimated that in one year the U.S. produced 1.3 trillion documents — enough to wallpaper the Grand Canyon 197 times.

- A survey developed by OfficeTeam found that 56 percent of 150 executives polled said the amount of paperwork in their office had diminished because of technological advances, whereas 44 percent believed the paper flow stayed the same or increased.

Source: www.os-od.com/updates/October/Paperless.html

of their accounting and financial systems, as well as production planning, manufacturing, inventory, and other control systems. Not only that, but many have made immense progress in computerizing other aspects of their day-to-day operations that involve documents. Plenty of efforts are underway that provide for electronic document management and what is called "workflow processing" within the corporate sector, particularly within large organizations.

Yet the internal focus of these efforts means that most companies operate inside a bubble — few have managed to extend the reach of their computer systems to the outside world. And so, while organizations might do a wonderful job in processing information internally, and might be making progress towards the paperless office in their internal handling of information, as soon as anything needs to go outside the organization — *wham!* It is printed out on paper.

Until recently, the cost of extending the reach of their systems to those with whom companies do business has been prohibitive, mostly because there hasn't been a way to easily link together different computer systems, or software to provide for inter-organization transactions. Companies in several industries did implement electronic data interchange (EDI) systems in the last decade, but the systems were cumbersome, technologically complex, and extremely expensive to put in place.

E-commerce Savings Begin Where Paper Ends

The Internet, however, suddenly provided the massive degree of connectivity required to support inter-organization transaction systems.

It is important that you understand what we mean by "connectivity." We're not referring to the fact that the Internet provides e-mail or lets someone link to a Web site of another organization. The connectivity we're talking about is much deeper than that, for it was now possible to develop systems that would permit an individual in one company to access the information and transaction systems of another company.

Once technology companies understood the massive connectivity that was available, they realized that therein lay an opportunity to develop software that would extend and link together business transaction systems. Implementing such systems would permit companies to re-engineer and streamline the way they did business with outside organizations, offering them the potential of saving money. That is why we have consistently said that one of the most significant e-biz opportunities focuses on cost reduction through the elimination of paper.

Why do electronic transaction methods offer cost savings? As with everything, some of the reasons are obvious, while others are not so obvious. For example, consider the process of billing, and the benefits that come from moving to an electronic invoicing system. The cost savings that result are due to the following:

> Jupiter Communications estimates that 74 percent of the $350 billion that will be spent on Internet infrastructure over the next three years will involve systems that streamline transactions between businesses and their customers.

- reduced need to create and mail paper invoices, with resultant savings in paper, postage, and staff time;
- faster reconciliation time to clear discrepancies in payment, through electronic access to information;
- cost savings that result from elimination of human error, which inevitably occurs when data is keyed in several times;
- less time spent chasing after the paper necessary to resolve a question, allowing discrepancies to be examined and followed up more quickly;
- better service response time through being able to immediately call up all the details of an electronic bill, rather than having to chase down the paper files, enabling supplier or customer questions to be answered much more quickly;
- cost savings resulting from not having to store paper.

The issue of dealing with errors and exceptions offers the biggest potential cost savings. In one study to support its efforts to move to electronic billing, IBM found that about 7 percent of paper invoices submitted by suppliers had to be returned and resubmitted because of errors. That involved extra time and, hence, extra money. An obvious benefit of electronic billing is the ability to instantly reroute an electronic bill back to a supplier, asking them to correct the error. The supplier can quickly make the corrections and resubmit the bill for payment. The Internet makes it even easier to deal with such matters, since it provides for instant routability of information via the Web and e-mail.

Migration from paper-based transaction systems to electronic ones is a business opportunity that makes sense. Cost-cutting has always been an important means by which a company can improve its bottom line. Indeed, the returns from cost-cutting can be dramatic. Imagine that a medium-sized company wants to increase its profit by $100,000. If it has a 10 percent return on its sales, it would have to increase sales by $1 million to achieve that goal, which could be a significant increase. Or it could figure out a way to save $100,000, with the same impact on the bottom line.

That's why e-commerce projects oriented towards cost reduction are likely to be a major area of focus within the corporate sector over the next several years. Evidence suggests that, as an organization implements electronic Internet-based transactions, it can reduce its day-to-day cost of doing business. Those savings flow right to the bottom line, in the form of profit.

OTHER BENEFITS OF ELECTRONIC STRATEGIES

As you try to figure out your opportunities in this area of the wired economy, you should have a good sense of the key corporate strategies that are being pursued. This can help to clarify the nature of the opportunity. Keep in mind that what we talk about here are the *potential* benefits that can come from strategies. How long it might take to achieve these benefits, if they are attained at all, is an open question.

- **Cost savings and operating efficiencies.** With the emergence of electronic transaction systems, companies are being presented with an opportunity to put in place computer systems that will, over time, offer cost savings and operating efficiencies. As we have seen, it costs a lot of money to move paper around. The Internet and the emergence of e-biz change that, because they permit organizations to interact electronically in a wide variety of ways, thereby achieving cost savings in their day-to-day interactions.

- **Significantly increased speed.** Not only will electronic transactions enhance cost savings and efficiency, they will help companies to operate faster, with such practical impacts as billing and receiving payments from customers on a much more timely basis. Conversely, of course, it will mean that they will be expected to pay their suppliers in a shorter time frame. Overall, many financial experts believe that the Internet is going to lead to a reduction in the "float," the length of time between when a company bills and when it collects, or when it is billed and when it pays.

- **"Electronic glue."** Electronic transaction systems offer an opportunity for companies to build long-term customer relationships that involve a form of "electronic glue." This is a significant point, and one that is often the least understood amid all the hype about B2B marketplaces. Some people think that e-biz opportunities are all about companies throwing existing relationships out the window in order to participate in an online marketplace, which will offer them cost savings through purchasing from a wide variety of organizations.

We think differently, as do many executives that we deal with. E-biz technology lets a company build electronic bridges to those with whom it has existing business relationships, whether they are suppliers or customers. It is about making existing relationships — and new relationships that come along — work better.

Setting up this form of electronic interaction allows a company to provide better service to customer organizations through the transactions between them. It makes sense to pursue a business strategy that offers such an excellent level of interaction and service that customers will be unlikely to take their business elsewhere. That's what we call electronic glue.

- **Instant interaction.** An electronic transactions strategy responds to demands by customers that their relationship with a company be enhanced through instant interaction. It is a defensive manoeuvre that responds to market realities. Examine the types of systems that companies are putting in place today, which permit customers and suppliers to make online account inquiries, initiate purchases, or undertake other types of transactions. Organizations are responding to the fact that many customers want such forms of interaction. Quite simply, they *must* do this in order to meet customer demands and expectations. We believe that companies that don't provide for such interaction in the future won't be enjoying the degree of market success they have today, simply because customers — whether they are consumers or business organizations — will have come to expect the ability to interact electronically as a standard service.

- **Marketing benefits.** The introduction of electronic transactions is an opportunity for companies to seek a competitive advantage by offering forms of electronic interaction that are not possible with their competitors. This is an important point as companies continue their search for methods of attracting new customers.

- **Resource reallocation.** Companies that have implemented effective transaction systems that reduce use of paper have found they can redeploy staff from routine tasks to more strategic and useful applications. In many organizations, sales staff are now involved in writing up routine orders, time that could be better spent working with the customer, trying to sell value-added or higher-margin items.

- **Partnering.** As a company extends the reach of its transaction systems, it can enjoy the benefits of industry partnerships. You will have noticed that everyone suddenly seems to be talking about the supply chain. They have become aware of the benefits of companies working together with their customers and suppliers, using as much electronic interaction as possible, through the entire process, from raw materials to final delivery of a product. The cost savings can be maximized and shared among all the participants. That is why we are seeing industry-wide efforts to automate business processes.

- **Better inventory management.** The ultimate goal of many of these efforts is to reduce inventory investment as much as possible and provide for better materials management. With inefficient ordering systems, companies have long had to ensure that they have adequate raw materials on hand for manufacturing purposes, or have needed excessive finished inventory on hand for sale to customers. But the experience of industries that have automated their transaction systems has led to the idea of "just-in-time" inventory. Electronic transaction systems are so fast and efficient that they can be used to generate orders just before the material or product is needed. The auto industry has shown that electronic transaction systems can have a massive impact on the level of inventory that needs to be carried. Since there is less money tied up in inventory, big savings flow through to the bottom line.

- **Improved budgeting and planning.** The inefficiency of paper-based systems, and the inherent delays they introduce into information processing systems, mean that organizations are often dealing with information that is out of date. Migration to the wired economy will slowly change that, allowing an improvement in forecasting and hence in the planning capabilities of organizations. And better forecasting and planning enable a company to better manage its finances.

- **Tighter production planning.** Another impact of electronic systems, for manufacturing companies in particular, is that better management of the ordering process helps to avoid production snafus. In a world in which production planning must be so tightly controlled and managed, the errors inevitably caused by paper-based systems lead to problems. Imagine a factory having to shut down the line for eight hours because someone reported that they had the 1,800 widgets necessary for production, but the actual number in stock was only 180. Because the company is working on incorrect information, it discovers the problem only when it runs out of widgets.

- **Better use of manufacturing capacity.** If a company can do better planning and forecasting, reduce errors, and move to just-in-time inventory, it can squeeze the most out of its production line.

Again, keep in mind that these are potential benefits of a move to electronic transaction systems. When these objectives are achieved, or whether they are achieved at all in a particular organization or, more broadly, within an industry, depends on time, the degree of effort put into the project, and many other factors. As we noted previously, the Internet doesn't happen overnight.

POSSIBLE OBSTACLES

We are also cautious about the time frame in which those potential savings might come about, because it takes a lot of effort to make electronic transaction systems work. But that is also where the business opportunities lie.

Opportunity will come about because these projects are more complex than people think, for all the reasons that we outlined in Chapter 1. Take the area of online purchasing. At the time we were writing this book (in early 2001), the National Association of Purchasing Management found that only 6.8 percent of its members felt they had made headway with e-commerce, since they were using the Internet for up to 40 percent of their purchasing. This means that 93 percent had barely even begun to get involved with e-purchasing. Not only that, but half of them indicated they had no plans to use the Internet for purchasing! And only a third reported that the Internet was a "very important" part of their future purchasing plans. The results of this survey also indicated that the group's members didn't agree that cost savings come about as quickly as touted; only 27 percent of the companies surveyed found they had achieved savings by using the Internet for purchasing.

Obviously, the things we talk about in this chapter are quite complex, and there are many reasons why it takes time to implement electronic transaction systems, and why organizations have not aggressively pursued the opportunities in front of them:

- **E-business software often has limited functionality and poor integration capabilities.** Many companies have rushed to adapt existing financial, transaction, or other software to support Internet and e-biz capabilities, and have often done an inadequate job. The result has been buggy software that has problems or is still too difficult to implement and modify. New e-biz software has been rushed to market, with similar results. When companies attempt to use this software to streamline the way they conduct business with the outside world, they can run into any number of problems.

- **Fears over downward pressure on pricing and other issues inhibit adoption of new ways of doing business.** Many e-biz initiatives that involve electronic transaction systems involve new business models or new ways of doing business within a marketplace. Often this can result in stress within an industry, since some will perceive new initiatives as threats (which is often the case). Take e-marketplaces, which usually involved some form of electronic transaction. Many of them died a quick death, since suppliers quickly realized that the impact of an e-marketplace would be to destroy their profit margins on the sale of goods or services. They would hardly be expected to support such efforts, and their attitude helped bring about the demise of many a marketplace. Implementation of a new system that might bring cost savings is often viewed with suspicion — by parties who presume that those savings are going to come out of their profits!

- **Skepticism abounds over benefits and cost savings.** Anyone remotely involved with the Internet is aware of a constant flood of predictions and statistics about potential cost savings. Indeed, we use some of those numbers in this book. Yet many people are rightly suspicious of the estimates — there often seems to be no rhyme or reason as to how they were figured out. Research companies releasing such statistics rarely divulge the methodology behind their numbers, which helps to raise suspicion still further. Hence, a lot of companies hold themselves back from pursuing electronic transaction systems, because they simply don't believe in the potential cost savings.

- **The cost of training and policy/process changes is a barrier.** Anyone involved in the implementation of computer systems knows that it can take quite some time to help staff understand how to use new systems. In addition, the implementation process can require substantial effort to ensure that it takes into consideration any special policies or processes already in place. This fact makes the implementation of systems more complicated than it might appear at first glance.

SIGNIFICANT PROJECTS ALREADY UNDERWAY

In light of all these obstacles, and especially given our previous skepticism about figures from the early days about the Internet and e-biz, your first reaction might be that the cost savings we talk about are ephemeral. They could be make-believe, part of the hype of the Internet/e-biz world.

Certainly this area of e-biz is already the subject of hype and, as with anything, estimates of overall cost savings and efficiencies should be taken with a grain of salt. Sometimes there is too much hype. Larry Ellison of Oracle has been quoted over and over again as saying that their e-biz systems have saved the company a billion dollars a year so far. There are those who quibble with the claim:

Microsoft's Goffe said he had examined Oracle's financial statements posted on its Web site and filed with the SEC. While there was indeed a $1 billion difference between Oracle's revenue growth and expense growth, the biggest decrease in expenses was in the services arena, he said.

"They saved $400 million in getting rid of people, not in savings they can directly attribute to their E-Business software," Goffe said.

"MICROSOFT, ORACLE BICKER OVER A BILLION,"
IN "EWEEK," *ZDWIRE,* FEBRUARY 20, 2001

Microsoft and IBM

Whatever their opinion on Oracle's e-biz, Microsoft has embarked on one of the most significant electronic billing projects around, and is eager to tout its success to anyone who listens. Microsoft has also been an aggressive implementer of extended accounting systems, through its MS Invoice initiative. This system permits suppliers to the organization to submit their invoices electronically rather than via the traditional paper route.

The results? The organization reports that it has driven the handling cost of each invoice from $19 down to $4. No wonder — it reduced the average time required to get an invoice into the system from 30 minutes to less than three minutes, with an average error rate of less than one percent. It also reduced the payment time from an average of three weeks down to only a few days. There were other benefits, too, such as reduction of administrative support staff required for payables from 25 people to 7 people. That represents big realized cost savings.

> You can read about the MS Invoice initiative online at www.microsoft.com/business/HowMicrosoftWorks/casestudies/msinvoice.asp

There are many other stories of companies who have successfully used the Internet to streamline the way external business transactions are conducted. IBM is getting close to a process that is 100 percent paperless for the majority of the invoices it receives from suppliers of goods and services. The company is very aggressive in working towards that goal; in June 2000 it began rejecting paper invoices from companies it knew were configured to submit invoices electronically. Globally, the company was 95 percent electronic by the end of 2000, with a goal of 98 percent by year-end 2001.

Beyond the Tech Sector

Such efforts are not restricted to tech companies. Consider the oil patch: Chevron is involved in an aggressive e-commerce project, the objective of which is to move many of their current paper invoices over to an electronic method of billing and payment. They expect to accrue savings of $240 million once they have managed to implement the system.

Even the advertising industry is getting involved in the move to paperless transactions. Members of the American Association of Advertising Agencies (www.aaaa.org), which includes such organizations as J. Walter Thompson, Young & Rubicam, Ogilvy & Mather, and DDB Worldwide, have agreed to stop receiving paper invoices from radio stations and move over to electronic billing. Altogether, this represents some $9 billion in annual advertising spending that is moving to electronic systems. The goal behind such an effort? To save money.

Such thinking isn't restricted to business either. Governments are also aggressively promoting electronic transaction systems. But, while there is a lot of rhetoric from elected officials and government organizations about Canada's need to get aggressive about e-business, few of them are actually practising what they preach. There are signs, however, that governments are getting ready to deploy large-scale e-commerce projects oriented towards cost savings. The Province of Ontario, for example, mandated in 2000 that they would move to electronic business within three years, their objective being to streamline transaction systems in order to save money.

SIGNIFICANT APPLICATIONS AND STRATEGIES
Now we've convinced you (we hope) that future efforts with the Internet and e-commerce are going to focus strongly on systems and initiatives that aim to reduce use of paper. So let's walk you through some of the types of applications that will play a key role in this process.

Electronic Bill-Payment Systems
One of the fastest growing e-commerce applications has to do with electronic bill-payment systems. You'll encounter a lot of information about this in the business world, the industry term being "electronic bill presentment and payment," or EBPP.

The concept of electronic billing is quite simple. Telephone, hydro, and other utilities, as well as department stores, credit card companies, and a host of other organizations, spend huge amounts of money sending out paper statements. They then expend a huge amount of energy on receiving payments on those accounts: processing the cheques, posting the payments, and following up on any errors in the process.

Electronic bill-payment systems promise a way to simplify that process. As a customer of a telephone company, for example, you may be asked to join their e-billing program, perhaps with some type of incentive for doing so (for example, a small discount on your bill). You are notified via traditional e-mail when an e-bill has been posted. You sign on to the Web site of the company that provides the e-billing infrastructure (such as Canada Post) and access your personal, private billing account. There you can examine the details of your statement, often in the same format as a paper bill. Since your billing account is linked to your bank account, you can simply press a few keys to instantly pay whatever you owe.

As e-billing evolves, several major companies will likely end up acting as e-billing clearinghouses. That is the role that organizations like

Canada Post and various banks are taking on with e-billing systems. Few billing companies will want to set up an entire e-billing infrastructure on their own; the complexity of integration into financial payment systems is far too complex. Hence, in order to access your bills, you'll sign into a mailbox with a clearinghouse organization that provides the e-billing infrastructure. You can learn more about e-billing by visiting Canada Post's EPOST Web site at www.epost.ca.

E-bill systems involve tight integration between corporate systems, financial institutions, and the electronic clearinghouses. Some major Canadian players are developing e-billing software, including Xenos (www.xenos.com) and Derivion (www.derivion.com); big players in the U.S. include CheckFree (www.checkfree.com). Browsing through the Web sites of these organizations is a very useful exercise that will help you better understand the electronic billing model, the market, and the opportunity.

There is a lot of excitement in the corporate world about the potential for electronic bill-payment systems, given that such significant potential savings can result from their deployment. Consider all the types of savings that can occur with e-billing, and you will understand why there is such excitement.

Printing and mailing expenses are eliminated. Studies suggest that it can cost from 75 cents to two dollars for the printing and paper-handling costs associated with each paper bill. Consider also the time and effort that go towards printing, folding, stuffing, metering, and sorting all those paper invoices, even when mechanical systems are involved, not to mention the postage to actually mail the bill. Companies can expect savings of anywhere from 20 cents up, depending upon the nature of the bill. Finally, there are the costs that can be reduced in processing the envelopes containing payment cheques and statement stubs, which are estimated to cost about $1.25 each to process.

> *Public Utilities Fortnightly* (www.pur.com/800.html), a publication for the utilities industry, estimates that $500 billion worth of U.S. utility bills will be sent by electronic billing systems by 2005.

Billing organizations, including government bodies, shell out three or four dollars per customer each month, or even more. An organization that has 100,000 customers could save $300,000 or more each year on mailing bills and collecting payment, if it can convince all of them to participate.

There are other reasons why e-billing is gaining so much notice. One of the big benefits of electronic bill presentment is that companies get their money a lot faster than they normally would. And there are marketing opportunities in using the Web site where the bill is presented to offer an advertising message tailored to specific customers.

> The banking industry currently renders about three billion paper statements and invoices each year.
>
> Source: *American Banker*, February 25, 2000

Jupiter Research (www.jup.com) suggests that we will see some two billion online bills being delivered by 2003, compared to 130 million in 1999. Another market research organization, PSI Global (www.psi-global.com), estimates some five billion consumer and business-related electronic bill payments annually by 2005, compared to just 21 million in 1999.

E-billing is going to take time to implement. As the history of the Internet has shown, it can take longer than expected for changes to occur, so the large-scale savings promised by e-billing may take some time to be realized. Old habits are hard to break, too — consumers don't like to change the way they do things. As we are writing this book, the reality is that most electronic billing applications have had only minimal adoption. We are nonetheless convinced that e-billing will be a major application in the world of business in the years to come.

Electronic Procurement and Tendering Systems

Another area that is being pursued is what has come to be called "e-procurement" (for electronic procurement) and electronic tendering/request-for-quote systems. Once again, the goal of the initiative is to "make the paper go away," thereby achieving cost savings through the resulting efficiencies.

Keep in mind that the benefits of such systems won't occur overnight, nor will implementation be as straightforward as some of the hype might suggest. E-procurement has received a tremendous amount of promotion and, in fact, has almost achieved the "next big thing" status that we've ridiculed in this book. Having said that, however, we still believe that it is an important opportunity.

What is electronic procurement and why are companies adopting the practice? E-procurement involves the electronic ordering of goods and services. In effect, companies are moving away from paper-based purchase orders, requests for quotes, and other methods of obtaining products or services, and moving to sophisticated electronic purchasing systems. It's like online shopping, except the transactions occur between business organizations.

The degree of sophistication of such initiatives, of course, varies. Some companies make a tepid effort by placing a form on their Web site that permits business customers to place orders. The form is not linked to the information systems of the organization, however, so they have really accomplished very little. More sophisticated systems allow the customer to enter a purchase order directly into the computer system of the supplier. A purchasing manager, for example, could visit the Web site of a key supplier, inquire into the inventory status of a particular part, and then place an order for that part directly into the supplier's system. In this way, the paper purchase-order process is eliminated, resulting in cost savings.

Many organizations throughout the world are pursuing such e-purchasing initiatives, and more can be expected to follow, as this application makes good business sense. An excellent example is found with GE Plastics (www.geplastics.com). Spend some time browsing through the many business divisions of this organization — such as the Bayer Silicones division shown on the following screen — and you will find a company that is aggressively involved in e-procurement. The home page for their services gives you an idea of the breadth of what they are doing online:

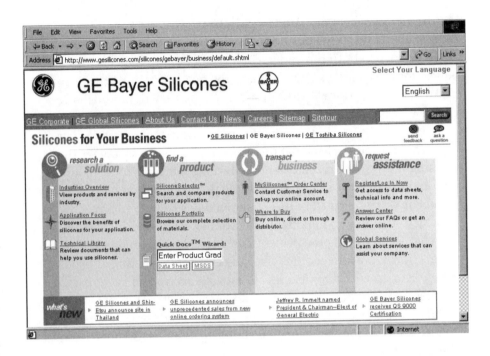

In Canada, Grand & Toy has been energetic in its implementation of an electronic purchasing system that allows its corporate customers to purchase office supplies online. By mid-2001 the organization was reporting that more than a third of their corporate business was being done through their Web site, with some $100 million in sales. The benefit to them is overall decreased costs, while their customers enjoy greater efficiency and their own cost savings.

However, e-procurement need not be restricted to simple purchase orders. Early on with e-commerce, many organizations came to realize that the Internet would offer a remarkable way for business or government organizations to issue electronic requests for quotes or tenders. A traditional practice in the world of business is the purchasing process in which companies put out tenders or requests for quotes — documents specifying their needs — to a large number of suppliers. They ask for a price quotation for the product or service in question and in this way can obtain a number of different quotes and, based on price and other factors, make their selection of whom to purchase from.

Not surprisingly, this aspect of the purchase process has moved on to the Internet. One of the best examples is the Canadian government's MERX system (www.merx.com), which allows federal and provincial government departments to issue tenders related to the purchase of goods and services. Since registration is not required, you can visit the site to get a good sense of how such systems work. (Note that you can't submit your own tenders to MERX. You can only use it to find tenders that have been issued by these government bodies.) Merely specify the type of product or service that you want to search for; in this case, we're looking for any tenders relating to oil. MERX responds with a list of current outstanding tenders that have been issued, with the date the tender was first placed online, the date it closes (when bids must be received), and the title/category that the tender fits within:

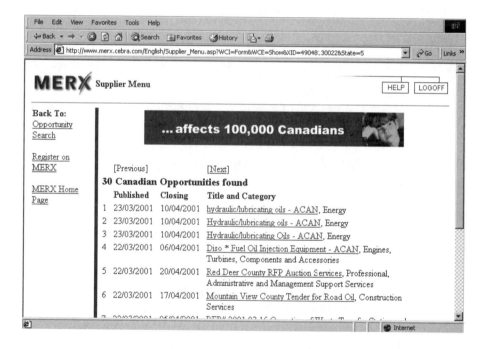

You can then examine the details of specific tenders by choosing any item from the list.

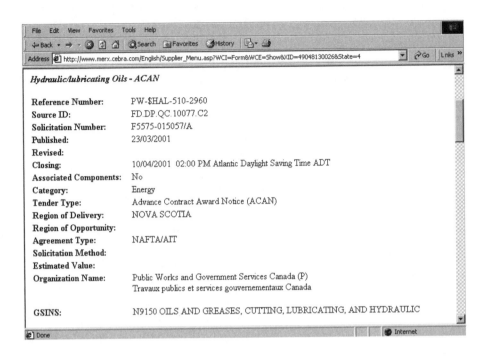

MERX is an excellent example of an online tendering application, and it is certainly successful. It is estimated that some $8 billion worth of business is tendered on the site each year, and that there are usually 1,800 open tenders on the site worth at least $25,000.

What are the benefits of e-procurement? Certainly there are the potential cost savings to be accrued over time as older, inefficient, paper-based systems are eliminated. In an article in *Electronic Commerce World*, Hudson's Bay Company noted that their electronic purchasing initiative provides them with three distinct benefits. First, they foresee a reduced cost in the process of issuing and managing purchase orders. Second, they believe it will lead to reduced inventory as a result of being able to order more quickly. And third, there are potential cost savings from reduced data-processing errors caused by multiple keying of data.

The key to making e-procurement work and achieving the cost savings is to ensure that any initiatives are integrated into the information systems of both the supplier and the purchaser. In the case of Grand & Toy, they have linked their Web site directly to their inventory and other financial systems. This means that the customer's order is going directly into the system, avoiding the need for data to be entered multiple times. That's key to achieving the cost savings that e-procurement presents.

As we noted earlier, it takes time to achieve the benefits of any e-biz application. However, there is already plenty of evidence that companies that successfully implement sophisticated e-procurement initiatives see savings. Dean Foods, based in Rochester, New York, began using an e-procurement system for purchasing maintenance, operational, and repair supplies. The objective was to reduce reliance on phone calls and faxes in the ordering process, and to avoid multiple entry of data. They reported significant savings:

The company was surprised to realize a nearly 75-percent time savings after implementing the new system.

"MAINTENANCE PROCUREMENT GOES ON-LINE TO REDUCE COSTS, SPEED PROCESSES AT DEAN FOODS," *MANUFACTURING SYSTEMS*, JUNE 1, 2000

Schlumberger's Diamant-Berger division estimated that it costs about $50 to $150 in wages to process the paperwork involved in a typical order — that is, the preparation of the order, routing it to appropriate parties for approval, and filing it. They pursued an e-procurement initiative because they figured it would cost only about $10 to $20 to do the same type of thing electronically, numbers that they now believe have proven themselves.

Another important reason why e-procurement will become more significant is that it allows companies or organizations to combine and centralize their purchasing power in order to drive down the cost of purchasing. Rather than having each of multiple divisions ordering products, they can combine their purchasing efforts. The increase in order quantity can help drive volume discounts, and the cost savings from this aspect of e-procurement can be significant. Unilever, a worldwide, $48-billion manufacturer of food, personal care, and home products, is working to centralize the purchasing activities of over 300 subsidiaries in 88 different countries. They estimate that consolidating their computer and information-technology spending is already leading to savings of $32 to $64 million in computer costs.

But while we believe the savings potential is real, we also fear that many organizations pursuing e-procurement and tendering initiatives will underestimate the cost and complexity of e-procurement systems. As we noted earlier in our chapter about Internet myths, the technology might be straightforward, but the implementation is not.

Customer Self-service Transaction Systems

Similar to e-procurement are the many initiatives that allow a customer or supplier to initiate a transaction with another organization, or to inquire about their account status with that organization. Some of these initiatives are designed to "make the paper go away," but they often go beyond that premise by reducing the interaction of people outside an organization with company staff.

In a world of extended accounting systems and wired supply chains, consumers and business organizations have come to expect to be able to examine the status of just about any interaction, or take a look at their history with the company, at just about any time. Providing such a capability certainly achieves cost elimination through the reduction of paper-based systems. That is why we are seeing huge growth in the number of organizations that are providing access to account and transaction details through their Web sites. When you allow the customer access to this information directly via your Web site, you can make significant savings because they are not tying up expensive human resources to resolve a simple inquiry.

Federal Express (FedEx) learned this lesson in the early days of the Internet. They quickly came to realize that if customers could find out the status of a shipment through a Web site, they wouldn't have to call in, using the more expensive resources of an 800 number. Hence, their strategy became to drive simple customer queries over to the Web and away from other, traditional channels.

With the rapid evolution of the Internet, interaction expectations quickly went beyond simple online status inquiries. Today people want to know not only the status of an order, but also details on whether it has been shipped, whether a partial order has been sent, and other similar details. They also want to access details on their accounts, including all charges and credits, and other types of information — on a regular, ongoing basis. Not only that, they want to be able to initiate business transactions. Companies are thus going to experience demands to open up their systems to permit such interactions. This is already underway in many organizations, and we believe that, over the long term, it will be a requirement of doing business for almost every organization.

A very good example of the type of online interaction that will become standard is found in the activities of Progressive Insurance, the fourth-largest U.S. underwriter of auto insurance (in 2000, they underwrote $6.1 billion in premiums). They have given customers extensive self-service capabilities at their Web site, personal.progressive.com. Online customers can access both policy and claims information, as well as a detailed resource centre, as seen on the following screen:

The service offered is quite sophisticated. Through the site, customers can make online policy updates, check claims status, access past claims, and determine how a claim will affect their rate. On the following screen, the customer is examining details of a specific policy. Progressive allows the customer to try out various scenarios with a policy, such as adding another vehicle or changing the amount of coverage. In addition, the customer can update any information with respect to the policy.

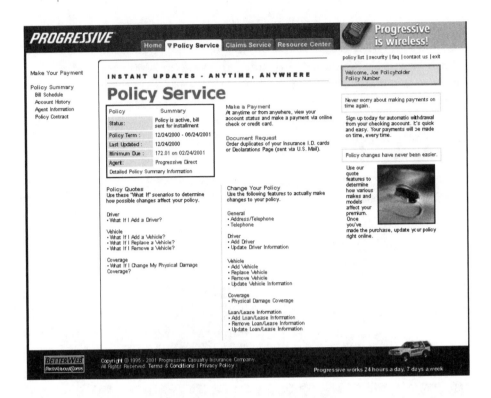

If the customer has a claim to make, they can provide full details online, and later they can read up-to-date information about the status of the claim. They can also learn what they can do while the claim is in process. For example, since these claims involve cars, people can find out what rights they have with respect to renting a replacement car. Each screen about a customer's claim is customized to the situation at hand.

Progressive's customers can also make online payments and authorize electronic funds transfer (EFT) withdrawals, as seen on the following screen:

They can also request additional insurance cards and copies of their declarations page, which are sent via U.S. mail. All told, the site offers policyholders a significant number of information resources.

Progressive also has a site for their agents, www.ForAgentsOnly.com, where agents can access policy details and submit endorsements (that is, obtain binding insurance coverage) online. This allows them to make policy changes very quickly, compared to the typical five or ten minutes that it takes via the phone. With such a tool, agents can examine a policy and process any necessary changes, thus instantly advising customers of rate changes. The site helps them to provide better customer service and streamline the transaction process. The following screen gives you an idea of the types of activities agents can undertake:

ForAgentsOnly.com Progressive-co Serv Cleveland,OH

Search FAQ: [   ] GO

Contact Us Site Map
Help Log Off

| Home | Policy Access | Production Numbers | Update Your Info. | Agent Forum | ProRater Support | Marketing | Progressive News | Technology |

Online Policy Access allows you to complete online endorsements, quote policy changes and view policy documents.

POLICY INFORMATION FOR AGENT CODE:

To logon, enter the following information for the policy you want to view or change.
(Please note that your agent code must match the agent code on the policy.)

1 Enter the policy number (e.g. 12345678-9):   [   ]

2 Policy changes will be emailed to: [   ]

3 Choose activity below:

(GO) **I WANT TO VIEW/CHANGE POLICY ***   AUTO, SPECIAL LINES   *Not all endorsements are available at this time. More Information

(GO) **I WANT TO VIEW DOCUMENTS**   AUTO, SPECIAL LINES, COMMERCIAL VEH

(GO) **I WANT TO VIEW CLAIMS INFO**   AUTO, SPECIAL LINES, COMMERCIAL VEH

○ **I WANT TO LOGIN UNDER A NEW AGENT CODE**

Note: Because we update our records from 2:00am - 4:00am (EST) Monday-Saturday and 12:00am - 8:00am (EST) on Sunday, Online Policy Access will not be available during this time period. Inquiries during this period will result in an error message.

Agents can also access their "production numbers," in order to review how they are doing in terms of commissions, policies written, sales performance, and other matters of importance:

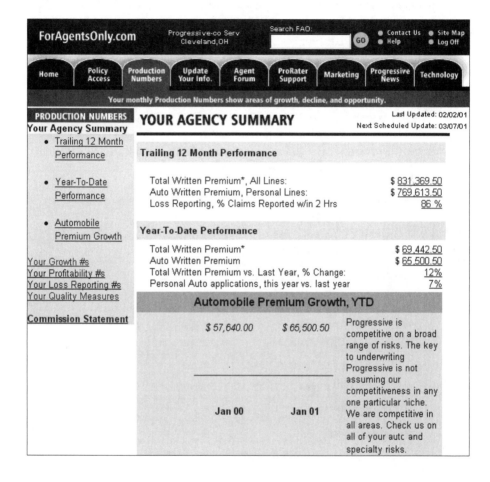

Progressive hasn't limited their online agent interaction to just these areas. They have also provided methods by which agents can access records that will help them manage a policy, including claims information, billing schedules, driving records, and account histories, thus helping them assess insurance coverage and renewals. And if they bind coverage for a customer online, they can even view and print the actual policy documents in order to provide them to the customer immediately.

That's an example of the type of interaction that helps a company excel at cutting costs and improving service, and which we believe will become standard for many organizations over time. An important point is that it isn't just business organizations that provide such online interaction; governments too are getting involved. A very good example is found with the North Carolina Web site:

The site is organized by the categories of questions people might have, unlike the typical government site, which is often organized by department. This is an important point. When you visit many government Web sites, they do not seem to offer much in the way of assistance. Rather, they seem designed to educate you on how that particular government is structured — or how wonderful it is! Contrast the previous screen to this one from the Province of Ontario, which seems to be little more than a press release for the party in power:

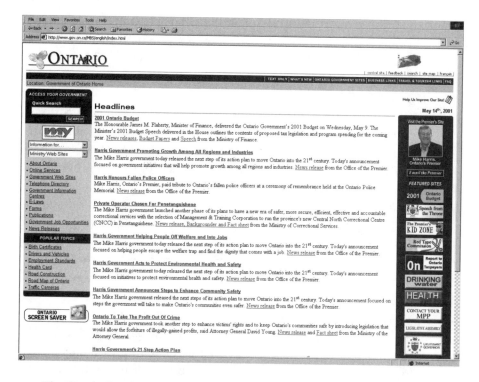

The North Carolina government Web site is also planning to support interactive transactions, similar to the type seen earlier with Progressive Insurance. Citizens will be able to inquire as to tax balances, as well as pay taxes, take out licences and other types of permits, and carry out just about any other type of transaction that they do with the state today.

We can expect to see massive levels of online interaction over the years to come, and the impact will be dramatic. Consider the way that you deal with a bank. If you are renewing a mortgage, you spend a great deal of time talking with your bank and sending back and forth the necessary forms, for example, appraisal updates and other information. Yet the Mortgage Bankers Association in the U.S. estimates that, within five years, up to half of all mortgage renewals could occur via the Web. They also believe that this will cause a 50 percent reduction in the costs of processing those mortgages.

We are going to see a flood of efforts by organizations to drive simple customer transactions over to Web sites. If you can get the customer to do the work, they believe, there is money to be saved.

THE NEXT STEP

While some of the activities described above offer wonderful cost savings, focusing on them can give you a rather limited view of how significant a change is coming to the business world. Some of the corporate sector's efforts so far don't truly take advantage of the opportunities of e-biz, in that many organizations will be implementing only fairly limited e-biz systems. For example, companies getting involved with e-procurement systems are often doing so on an extremely limited basis, in that all they will do is allow people to submit purchase orders online. Then they'll simply plug those orders into the already paper-intensive systems in place, and thereby will see little of the cost savings that real e-biz offers.

Organizations that move beyond simple e-procurement or other straightforward applications will realize that the biggest e-biz opportunities come from extending the reach of their various financial and transaction systems to their customers, suppliers, and other business partners. While the vast majority of businesses have computerized accounting, financial, and other transaction systems, few of them have expanded those systems to include their customers and suppliers. But if they do so, they will be able to realize significant operating efficiencies, since such efforts also help to make the paper go away. Helping to bring about this new era of online interaction are fundamental changes to the very nature of the financial, production planning, and other software being used by the corporate sector.

Extended Accounting and Transaction Systems

It isn't a stretch to state that much of the transaction software used by business, in both large and small organizations, is being modified to permit interaction via the Web with the software and with the data behind it. We call this the world of extended accounting and transaction systems.

How might such an extended system work? Consider a company that carries an inventory of tens of thousands of parts. Up-to-the-minute details on the quantities of each part in stock are maintained within the inventory portion of the company's financial accounting system. Customers might want to know if a particular type of product is in stock. What happens? They dial an 800 number and talk to a customer-service representative, who types the query into the inventory system.

What a waste of time! Think about it — the company could have several people dedicated to taking such calls. Wouldn't it be better if the customer could access a Web site to submit the query? And then place the order directly through the Web site, if so inclined? In effect, the customer would be interacting directly with the company's financial system and initiating the transaction, thereby avoiding the more labour-intensive older method.

To accomplish this, the company would have to be able to link its inventory and purchase-order systems to the Internet. Given trends in the world of accounting software, this is becoming an increasingly more straightforward process. A very good example of the technology that allows companies to extend the reach of their financial systems is found with AccPac accounting software (www.accpac.com), which is aimed at small and medium-sized enterprises. AccPac features a range of accounting modules, including systems for inventory, accounts payable, receivables, billing, purchasing, and other activities. The company boasts a client base of hundreds of thousands of organizations worldwide.

With the emergence of the Internet, AccPac realized that there was an opportunity for users of their systems to get into e-business simply and effectively — by extending those systems to the outside world via the Web. They developed what they call eTransact, a set of software modules that allows AccPac users to link their financial and other transaction systems directly to a corporate Web site, giving customers direct access to the data within these systems, and to interact with that data.

What could a company using AccPac do with the eTransact software? Exactly what we have described above — link its inventory system to its Web site, and thus permit customers to make inquiries about inventory status and then order the product directly. Such efforts aren't restricted to AccPac; every major producer of accounting, financial, transaction, product-planning, or other software has developed or is working on similar capabilities for their systems to be linked to the Web.

Consider SAP (www.sap.com), J. D. Edwards (www.jdedwards.com), and PeopleSoft (www.peoplesoft.com). Together, these organizations provide software that fuels the accounting/financial systems of tens of thousands of companies worldwide. They too have invested heavily to provide capability for the Web to be linked to the data that exists within these systems. This capability allows companies to implement a wide range of functions that extend the reach of their accounting and transaction systems.

But are companies exploiting these opportunities? Some are, but many other organizations have not. Some haven't yet strategically identified this as an area where they should be spending their time. Companies in the high-tech industry have come to realize that they need to do a tremendous amount of education to help senior business strategists understand the implications of extended accounting and transaction systems.

There is no doubt that the emergence of such a fundamental change in the systems that make up our financial and transaction world will result in a tremendous number of opportunities involving the strategic design and implementation of such technology.

Supply-Chain Reorganization

The real implication of extended accounting and transaction systems is that, in many sectors, particularly those involving the manufacture or supply of products, we are going to see massive reorganization and integration of the supply chain.

The ultimate strategy of the interconnected business world is to intertwine the financial, production, and manufacturing systems of an organization to such a degree that manufacturers and their suppliers can work together. How might e-commerce work in this context? Let's move beyond the simple inventory/purchase-order concept that we've outlined above.

In a supply chain, the customer might initiate an order with a manufacturer for a certain number of products. That automatically triggers the manufacturer's production planning systems to signal its suppliers to ship only a specific quantity of necessary supplies, since it doesn't want to bear the cost of keeping excess inventory on hand. Once the supplies arrive, they are automatically entered into the production system. The manufactured products are then sent to the customer along with an electronic invoice.

The backbone for this type of system? The Internet and the e-commerce tools that permit a massive level of integration between various financial, transaction, manufacturing, and other systems. The objective of supply-chain projects is to lower inventory carrying costs by holding less inventory, and to provide for far more efficiency within the overall industry between buyers and sellers, thus reducing costs for all parties. There is some debate as to whether those objectives might ultimately be met, but they seem like worthy goals.

Supply-chain rationalization might sound a bit like science fiction to some people, but in certain industries, such as auto manufacturing and electronics, it has led to remarkable change. In fact, the concept of just-in-time inventory resulted from this type of system interaction within the auto industry, with the implementation of EDI, years ago. During the next 20 years, quite a few companies in a wide variety of industries are going to feel the effects of similar supply-chain initiatives. Not surprisingly, a tremendous amount of effort will be going towards designing, implementing, and supporting such systems.

The move to use the Internet to reinvent the supply chain is happening with particular aggressiveness within the high-tech industry. There is a strong belief that the ultimate goal of extended transaction systems should be to get a better handle on supply-and-demand issues, so that an organization can do a better job in production planning. One of the leaders in this area is Analog Devices (www.analogdevices.com). They're working beyond the process of merely taking an order through a Web site, by ensuring that they link every internal system, from product design and manufacturing management to shipping and logistics, to the Web. This allows all their partners to interact with them throughout the process.

Supply-chain redesign involves a complete and fundamental rethinking of the business process of an organization, and of the way it does business with its partners. Companies like Analog Devices are doing that today:

"Our emphasis in terms of E-business is fundamentally rethinking and stream-lining the business processes and not just focusing on the mechanics of taking an order," Analog Devices' Loh says. "To do that, we have to work on systems integration, from the front office to the back office."

"SEMICONDUCTOR MAKERS AND SUPPLIERS ARE USING THE WEB
TO DECENTRALIZE OPERATIONS: CHIPMAKERS REACH OUT TO INTERNET,"
INFORMATIONWEEK, SEPTEMBER 11, 2000

The fascinating thing about Analog Devices and other high-tech companies is that they are starting down a road that will see tight linking of their financial systems, such as order processing and inventory, to the production planning systems that they use. Their goal is that they will be able to adjust their manufacturing levels and plans automatically, based upon actual orders received. They hope to be able to do this on a nightly basis, thus putting in place a very effective matching of supply and demand.

The concept of supply-chain rationalization is one of the fastest-growing business applications, and if you take the long view of five to twenty years, you can expect it to come to play an important role for most manufacturers. It is already gaining attention in major companies: A study by Zona Research (www.zonaresearch.com) in 2000 found that, of 100 major companies examined, 25 had implemented some type of supply-chain automation, another quarter planned to do so by the end of 2000, and the balance would be putting it in place throughout 2001. This means that, far from being theoretical, supply-chain rationalization is already and definitely a real application.

NEW MARKET REALITIES

There is plenty yet to come with e-biz as corporations wake up to opportunities for streamlining their business activities through use of the Internet. When you have finished this chapter, you will appreciate that the business world is facing an unprecedented opportunity in the way it might use technology.

By and large, however, while many organizations are in the midst of projects such as those described in this chapter, the vast majority have yet even to consider, let alone begin, their undertakings in this area. In a way, this isn't surprising. It has long been a truism of the computer era that it takes organizations a long time to perceive the strategic opportunities and possibilities that can come from the deployment of technology. It takes even longer to deploy and successfully implement sophisticated technologies, and longer still to enjoy a payback.

Given the period of dot-com hype that we recently experienced, many executives and organizations today are somewhat skeptical of *anything* involving the Internet and e-commerce. And so, even as some organizations charge ahead, many will be left behind. In the short term, this might not mean much. But we are convinced that, in the long term, organizations will be forced to participate in many of the activities described in this chapter in order to stay competitive. The move towards the elimination of paper exchange and paper-based transaction systems is something that will be required of every organization.

We have noted that this transition will be triggered by customer expectations — quite simply, people will come to demand these capabilities. But there is also a more subtle change at work here. As we explained earlier in this chapter, many e-commerce projects are being pursued with the basic premise that they represent an opportunity to save significant sums of money. After all, goes the theory, an electronic transaction is far less expensive to process than its paper counterpart. Fewer staff are involved in routing the transaction, not to mention the savings that can be made from reducing the use of paper, including the necessity for filing cabinets and the other infrastructure associated with paper-based ways of doing business. (Companies in the electronic document business have done some fascinating studies on the cost of paper storage!)

During the next several years, e-commerce projects whose primary purpose is cost savings will be some of the most significant activities underway throughout the economy. This activity is going to lead to some significant new challenges for plenty of organizations, particularly those who don't get involved, because their competitors will be able to undercut them on price.

The recent history of business is littered with the wreckage of companies that have not managed to squeeze productivity gains using computer technology. Often this has come about because of poor implementation of the technology, while in other cases they simply chose not to pursue such projects, often because they failed to understand the strategic opportunity in front of them. By not effectively implementing technology when their competitors were, they ended up with a higher cost structure.

So it is with e-commerce. Some companies will aggressively pursue electronic commerce projects and will be able to reap the benefits that come from successful implementation. They will reduce their cost of doing business and will be able to pass some of those cost savings on to their customers, in the form of reduced prices.

But plenty of companies won't pursue cost-saving e-biz opportunities as quickly or as successfully, or they won't bother with it at all. Those companies will be faced with a higher cost structure and more administrative overhead, and other associated costs that come from being stuck in the paper age. They will discover, only too late, that suddenly their competitors can undercut their prices to a greater degree because they can pass on their cost savings. Obviously, should they be unable to catch up over time, they will find themselves in a dangerously uncompetitive position.

Is the opportunity real? We will leave you with some closing thoughts. Consider some numbers from an article that appeared just when the 2001 recession seemed to be getting underway:

Companies are plowing ahead with Internet technology investments despite the economic slowdown, citing cost and competitive pressures as well as longer-term strategic positioning. At the same time, IT executives are under closer scrutiny to prioritize Internet projects based on their expected returns.

"WHAT SLOWDOWN?: E-BIZ SPENDING STILL SOARING,"
INTERNET WEEK, JANUARY 22, 2001

The article went on to say that 77 percent of executives believed their Internet spending would increase in 2001; only 4 percent expected it to decrease. And most expected it would increase by an average of 40 percent. Indeed, eight in ten said that concerns about a slowing economy wouldn't affect their e-biz plans.

The projects these companies are working on, and the strategies behind their efforts, are precisely the things we have identified in this chapter. Jack Cooper, vice-president and CIO of Bristol-Myers Squibb, noted in the article that "companies want to improve responsiveness to customers, reduce inventory costs and reduce materials costs, and the Internet provides a marvellous collaborative tool to accomplish that." What is Bristol-Myers focusing on? Transaction efforts such as tools that provide for customer access and streamline its supply chain. Other companies in the article, such as Whirlpool, noted that they would be focusing on the same thing, also with the objective of cutting costs and improving external relationships.

Is e-biz real? You bet.

Chapter 5

The Customer-Centred Organization

Growing competition and globalization in the marketplace means the fight to retain customers is more challenging than ever. Gone are the days when companies could sit back and rake in the benefits of having a loyal band of customers without worrying about losing them to competitors offering a better service.

Nowadays, customers are far more fickle, and if businesses fail to provide a consistently effective, efficient service then people will simply go elsewhere. What is worse is that in the realm of e-commerce, a competitor may be just a few mouse clicks away.

"BUSINESS: THE CUSTOMER IS KING," *PC DEALER*, DECEMBER 13, 2000

IN THE NEW WORLD OF EXTENDED ACCOUNTING SYSTEMS AND ELECTRONIC supply chains that we described in the last chapter, the issue of customer support has become far more critical than ever before. In addition, as people come to rely on the Internet as a source of information for their purchasing decisions, providing quality service online has become critical.

While consumers might not yet be doing much shopping online, they expect to be able to interact with companies in a variety of ways, and to get effective support almost instantly. Furthermore, as organizations weave their operations into those of their business partners, the ability to resolve issues quickly has become a critical component of the relationship. These two facts mean that, over the next several years, we are going to see continued growth in what we might refer to as customer care and support applications. This is bound to be one of the most significant areas of opportunity within the wired economy.

CHANGING CUSTOMER EXPECTATIONS

One of the primary reasons why customer care and becoming a customer-centred organization are going to become so important is that the Internet has led to a massive spike in the expectations that customers have when it comes to customer service.

Almost-Instant Response

Given the 24/7 culture of the Internet, customers have come to expect to get answers to any question at any time — and quickly — from any organization they might be dealing with. By the end of 2000, according to Jupiter Research, 55 percent of online shoppers expected an answer to an e-mail question within six hours. But few companies seem to be able to live up to such expectations: The same survey showed that only 29 percent of Web sites were able to reply within such a short time.

Given this disparity, it isn't surprising that the survey also shows that 62 percent of those people are disappointed with online customer service. And things are going to become much worse. Jupiter estimates that, by the end of 2001, people will expect an answer to an e-mail question within an hour or less.

E-mail is fast becoming the communication method of choice for U.S. adults. Sixty percent of U.S. Internet users prefer reading their e-mails to reading ordinary postal mail, and 34 percent prefer to send e-mail rather than make a telephone call.

Source: AmericanGreetings.com, January 2000

Not only that, but people will be sending in a lot of support questions. A study by the Harris Poll found that 25 percent of Americans use e-mail on a daily basis, and that people are sending some 50 million product or service inquiries by e-mail *per day*. That's 50 million e-mail messages per day seeking answers to questions! We think this is an absolutely stunning number, particularly when people are coming to expect an answer within an hour.

Another telling statistic about customer-support demands brought about by the Internet comes from Forrester Research. They indicate that, by the end of 2001, some 20 to 30 percent of customer contacts will have shifted from telephone, fax, and regular mail over to the Web and e-mail.

The emerging flood of electronic mail queries from customers has presented most organizations with a significant problem. Indeed, it puts them between a rock and a hard place, to such a degree that they will have to ramp up their spending significantly in order to deal with the problem. Why is this so? Because few organizations have the information in a readily accessible format, and hence can't deal swiftly with customer queries. Never before have they had to deal with so much customer interaction, with customers asking such a wide range of complex questions, the answers to which are often not readily available even to staff. Sure, the information might exist within the organization, but much of it is probably not easily accessible via a computer. It's never been committed to an electronic database, never been organized, and indeed, has probably never even been "inventoried" to determine what information might exist.

Think about customer service prior to the Internet. Except for organizations that had effective, sophisticated 800-number call centres, there was often little interaction with customers. Telephone systems presented a psychological barrier that discouraged calling. Few people were willing to tackle a system in which they could be placed on hold forever, listening to lousy Muzak renditions of Beatles songs, and were even more reluctant to leave voice messages seeking assistance. Quite simply, despite advances with call centres, many people didn't like telephone support systems, since they could often be a frustrating experience. (To illustrate that, witness the complaints about Air Canada's call-centre support!) Fewer still would take the time to write a letter or send a fax to a company.

With the Internet, the dynamics of customer support are entirely different. People can surf from company to company in a matter of moments. They can ask their questions by filling out a form or sending an e-mail message. On

> 73 percent of customers chose e-mail as their first choice to receive customer service, followed by Web site self-help, in-person, and telephone.
>
> Source: *Socratic Technologies,* November 1999

sites that provide stellar levels of customer support, they've come to be what we might call "engaged customers" — who interact with companies far more than ever before.

This results in a big problem: The Internet has raised expectations to such a degree that companies cannot afford to slip up when it comes to customer service. They have no choice but to set up e-mail support and spend the money necessary to do it right. Otherwise, customers will quickly vent their frustrations by taking their business elsewhere. That is why, when it comes to future opportunities online, the area of customer care is likely to be one of the fastest-growing areas in the world of e-biz. Quite simply, scaling up to a world in which customers get the online support they want is going to cost a lot of time, effort, and money.

High Levels of Interaction

Online customer service doesn't just involve answering e-mail on time. The expectations of customers, regardless of whether they are private consumers or represent a business, have gone far beyond simple answers to queries. Today's sophisticated customers expect to be able to use the Internet in a number of different ways — most of which an organization might not be prepared to support — including access to documents, support databases, account inquiries, and online ordering.

Because the Internet has led to customers being able to interact with some organizations at all hours of the day, they are beginning to expect to be able to deal in the same way with all the companies with whom they do business. People have become quite aggressive as they search for answers to problems or for information that is relevant to their daily lives.

Let's put this into perspective with an example. Many people have signed up for electronic stock-trading services, such as E*TRADE and TD Waterhouse, or are actively pursuing online banking. They can sign in to such services at any time to undertake sophisticated financial activities such as buying and selling shares or online banking. They can access a wealth of documentation and information that assists them with the decisions and activities they want to undertake. Not only that, they can access up-to-date details on their accounts and trading activities at any time; the full history of their relationship with the organization is available to them.

This makes them wonder — why can't they do this with their insurance company, department store, or other organizations that they deal with? Why can't they find a product manual for their power drill? Why can't they find warranty information about something they bought from you, or determine whether they are still under warranty? This presents a challenge: While some companies, such as financial organizations, have lots of experience in extending their systems to their customers, few others do.

Competition Is Just a Click Away

You might think that companies could afford to opt out of providing online support. We think differently. From our perspective, the experiences that customers have with some online Web sites lead them to expect the same level of professional service from every organization that they deal with. For example, if someone buys a system from Dell Computers, whose site is known for its excellent online customer service, they will use Dell as the standard for judging customer service elsewhere.

Customers begin to wonder why they can't have the same level of service from every business, large or small. This means that, regardless of the organization, they come to expect an extremely high level of professional customer service — all the time, from every organization that they deal with.

However, few companies seem to have the mindset to cope with this aggressive new type of customer. Take the insurance industry: It has often been said that the biggest challenge an insurance organization faces is that it has precious little experience in extending the reach of its computer systems beyond the organization. Yet it is now faced with customers who expect a high level of online, transaction-based interaction, simply because they get such service from their banks. When you mix in the fact that insurance companies are increasingly finding themselves competing with banks, it becomes clear that they are going to have to spend heavily to provide the level of interaction that their customers demand.

A study in 2000 by Cahners In-Stat Group found that 82 percent of small businesses with fewer than five employees, and 61 percent of small companies (5 to 99 staff) indicated that the Internet has resulted in a need for improved customer service.

The same situation exists within many business-to-business relationships. Over the next several years, as companies extend their transaction systems and work to streamline their supply chains, they are going to have far more interaction with suppliers and customers than ever before. This means that people's expectations are being affected not only in their roles as consumers, but also in their jobs — they will expect to get stellar support from every organization they deal with. They will want to instantly determine the status of any order and find out its shipping status. They will demand to receive and pay for all transactions electronically. As manufacturing systems become bound to the Internet, they will expect to be able to determine the status of their order on the shop floor, or even become interactively involved, via the Internet, in the design and manufacture of the product they want to purchase.

Another important point is that people are developing the same expectations of government as they are of business. Anyone who has dealt with any level of government on just about any issue has been frustrated by bureaucratic processes, marginal service, and extensive waits to get resolution of even the most straightforward problem. But now, as more people are surfing the Web more often, they are coming to think they should be able to get the same level of online support from government as they do from the business sector. Indeed, some government organizations are even helping to set those higher expectations:

Historically, citizens' perception of government service has been less than glowing. When they think about the prospect of contacting the government in almost any way, they picture long waits and cumbersome procedures. The experience of interacting with government is nearly always foreseen as a frustrating chore.

"AT THE DAWN OF E-GOVERNMENT: THE CITIZEN AS CUSTOMER,"
GOVERNMENT FINANCE REVIEW, OCTOBER 1, 2000

Organizations cannot avoid the danger that this heightened level of expectation presents, because the existence of the Internet has shifted the balance of power over to the consumer. In many industries, the consumer has long been captive to the supplier — it hasn't been easy or convenient for them to explore alternatives. But now, with the Internet, they see that there aren't many differences among the competing products or services they might be purchasing. Someone buying a Lego set online for her children might be heavily influenced by price, shipping policies, and rates, and perhaps the brand name of the organization she is dealing with. But, by and large, at this stage of e-commerce there is often little difference when it comes to those factors.

> Sixty-nine percent left companies' Web sites and visited the sites of their respective competitors if they weren't pleased with the service they received online.
>
> Source: *Call Centre Magazine,* January 2000

This means that the deciding factor for many consumers, whether they are purchasing on the Internet or merely using it to research something they are planning to buy, will ultimately be the customer service and interaction they experience. That's where a well-established maxim of the Internet comes into play: "A competitor is just a mouse-click away." People can take their business elsewhere more easily than ever before. If a company doesn't excel at customer service and interaction, it will cause itself massive damage in the eyes of the buyer.

History has shown that if a company does not provide excellent customer care, the Internet can bite back! In all too many situations, customers who have encountered very poor support have used the Internet to vent their frustrations. That is why we have seen the emergence of so many corporate "suck" sites — Web sites where someone has taken the corporate name, has appended the word "suck" or a similar insult, and has used it to make others aware of their problems. This new form of consumer empowerment means that, should customers believe they have been wronged by a company, they often take into their own hands the opportunity to complain loudly.

For example, consider the aircanadasucks.com site, a unique method by which people can vent their frustrations, if they have any.

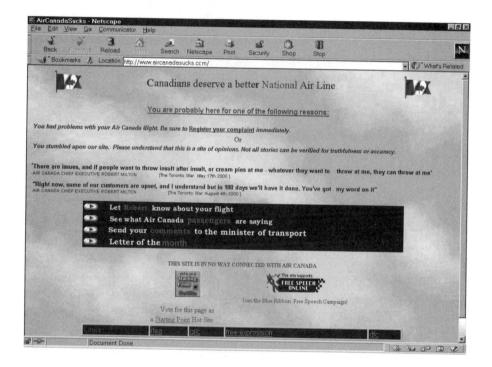

A Culture of E-support

We believe that it will take a lot of effort within companies to get all staff to understand and appreciate the role of the Internet in service delivery. Real support is something more than e-mail, information repositories, and online interaction. We believe that the Internet is creating such heightened expectations that every organization is going to have to become "customer-centric" — to develop a culture in which their very mission is to excel at dealing with the customer. They have a long way to go in this regard; few companies seem to be doing what is necessary to make such a cultural shift.

BENEFITS OF IMPROVED CUSTOMER CARE

There is no shortage of reasons for companies to pursue more sophisticated activities in the areas of customer care and interaction. Here are some of the key business objectives that we feel companies need to address in order to become customer-centred organizations.

- **Effective digital customer support.** An effective digital customer-support strategy responds to the market realities of today. In a world in which consumers and buyers have come to rely upon the Internet, there is growing expectation that a company must offer excellence in customer service. Organizations that are unable to do so will have a more tenuous relationship with their customers. A survey by NetCall, a U.K. company, found that 78 percent of consumers would take their business elsewhere if they had but one bad online transaction with a company.

  In the new era of e-biz, companies are faced with more competition than ever before, potential for shrinking margins on product or service sales, and customers that are far less loyal than ever before. Clearly, they must work harder to keep existing customers.

- **Significant cost savings.** You can do this by ensuring that customers contact you via more expensive traditional methods, such as an 800 number, only if they have been unable to take care of their concerns directly through your Web site. Indeed, it has long been recognized that cost savings are to be had by "getting the customer to do the work" as much as possible.

  Every time someone interacts with a customer-care centre to deal with a question or an issue, a more expensive resource has not been used. If a company approaches the issue of customer care correctly, it can ensure that only a very small percentage of customers actually phone in. By doing that, the organization can dramatically reduce the overall cost

---

PRINCIPLES OF SUCCESSFUL SELF-SERVICE

- Automate repeat problems with known solutions.
- Offer a user-friendly, intuitive interface that hides back-end complexity.
- Leverage, rather than replace, existing infrastructure.
- Ensure convenience by offering the solution at the point of the problem.

Source: www.courion.com

of customer support. Forrester Research estimates that handling customer support by e-mail costs about two-thirds less than an 800-number call centre, and that if the customers get the answers off the corporate Web site themselves and don't have to e-mail, it costs even less.

- **Feedback mechanisms.** By analyzing the documents that customers view and the types of resources they are using in the Web site, an organization can better determine how to respond to customer needs. Indeed, there may be no better way for an organization to learn about its customer relations and activities. It can review incoming e-mail support questions to determine if problems are occurring consistently with particular products or services. Search phrases might be reviewed to determine what customers are looking for — and to see if the Web site is providing effective answers. Inquiries about certain products at certain times of the year may result in special promotions or cross-selling of other products. In other words, an organization can learn a lot about its customers through an effective support strategy, and act accordingly.

- **Building customer loyalty.** Building customer loyalty means building better relationships with customers. Organizations that have effectively exploited the Internet by providing a high level of online service have found that it is an extremely powerful tool for building and enhancing those relationships. This is an important point in the era of the Internet, which is leading to greater "churn." McKinsey & Company found that 67 percent of Internet customers don't make repeat purchases; that is, they take their business elsewhere, demonstrating little loyalty to companies.

- **Freeing up corporate resources.** If an organization manages to create a truly effective customer-care site, it is freeing up valuable human resources that can better serve other functions. An organization might find that its sales or other staff are too wrapped up in dealing with routine support problems with their customers. A lot of time is wasted when they deal with things that could be more effectively addressed if customers used the Web to obtain answers or support. Additional time is spent doing routine order-taking with customers. Sales staff could, if freed from such chores, spend more time selling, which, of course, has a significant impact on the bottom line. Better yet, they could focus on providing more effective, value-added service to their customers. Or staff who have been spending a lot of time answering routine inquiries via an 800 number could be deployed to other, more productive tasks.

- **Capturing important corporate knowledge.** Dealing with customer-support issues can lead an organization down the path to creating a knowledge library. Quite often, the knowledge accumulated by people throughout the organization — about their products and services and solutions to problems that customers might encounter — is never documented or written down. In establishing a customer-care centre, an organization starts the process of capturing and harnessing this valuable knowledge so that it is not forever lost when individuals leave the company. Customer care thus assists the company in dealing with what has been dubbed "intellectual capital" (which is, as we will see, an extremely time-intensive project).

- **Public relations.** Finally, the customer-support centre becomes an important and effective public relations tool. If a company has an important message that it needs to get out to its customers, its customer-care centre can be an important means by which it does so.

WHY ARE COMPANIES FAILING AT ONLINE CUSTOMER SERVICE?

We've already mentioned that, when it comes to customer service, many organizations are doing a poor job. Internet-based customer support has already received a bad rap because of its poor execution by many a high-profile dot-com.

> Companies aren't failing just with Internet customer service. A survey by Siemens Communications found that, while 75 percent of people have called a customer-service number in the last three years, their satisfaction with that service has declined.

Many of the companies involved in early e-commerce were too caught up with other difficult e-biz issues, such as fulfillment and product returns, and hence didn't commit resources to customer service. It came almost as an afterthought, particularly after the disastrous 1999 Christmas season, during which customer dissatisfaction with online shopping reached an all-time high. What happened? People ordered goods, didn't receive them in time, and couldn't get answers from the online company as to when they might arrive. Orders, if they were shipped, were often incorrect. When people tried to return goods, they found that the company either lost the returns or was never set up to receive returned goods in the first place! Throughout the debacle, companies were unresponsive to their customers' queries, and the entire e-commerce industry earned a black eye as a result.

The sour taste that people got from online customer service has not been helped by the fact that, for many early dot-com organizations, their "exit strategy" had nothing to do with building a real, successful business. The goal of many dot-com entrepreneurs was to build a business quickly that they could sell to someone else, often at a high price. Take it public, cash out, get your money, and run! Such thinking meant that, in the grand scheme of things, customer service was unimportant, an expense that could be avoided and an issue that could be dealt with by someone else, later down the road. Sadly, when people are blinded by dollar signs, they never pay attention to the stuff that matters.

> Of 836 online consumers, 63 percent experienced long waits for replies to e-mail messages. Sixty-nine percent said automated replies to e-mail inquiries weren't helpful. Sixty-five percent identified lack of response to e-mail as a major problem.
>
> Source: *Call Centre Magazine*, January 2000

And so the early days of the e-biz revolution were less than pretty when it came to dealing with customers. Established, "real" businesses have had online customer-support problems as well; they haven't been restricted to dot-com start-ups. Like many users of the Internet, both the authors regularly experience the challenge of online customer support firsthand, and many of those situations, whether they have been with start-ups or with the Web sites and e-commerce activities of established companies, crystallize for us the nature of the problem.

> Only eight percent of 836 online shoppers surveyed reported having no problems using e-mail to obtain customer service.
>
> Source: *Socratic Technologies*, November 1999

Let's walk you through some of the problems we have encountered, and explain what has to happen within an organization in order to avoid them. That, more than anything, will help you understand why the issue of e-biz and Internet-based support is going to be so significant, and why it is going to present opportunities.

Failure to Get Staff "On Side"

Some years ago we began making our airline reservations online. We were being encouraged to do so by a particular airline, which was running full-page ads promoting their new Web-based booking system. One day we had a problem with a ticket, and called the central reservations number to get someone to deal with it. It quickly became apparent that the reservation agent was unfamiliar with the online system, and at one point she commented in frustration that we really shouldn't be using the Internet.

Out of curiosity, we asked her what she knew about the Internet. She admitted that she had never seen the Internet-based booking system, and had not been given any information about it. All she knew was that she was receiving an increasing number of calls from customers about online bookings, and when there were problems or questions about these bookings, she had no idea how to deal with them. And so, in her frustration, she began to tell the customers that they should go back to traditional ways of doing business with the company.

Think about what went wrong here. This situation suggests an organization that has established an e-biz strategy for perfectly valid business reasons (having customers do their own bookings saves money), but has implemented the strategy inside a bubble. They carried through on the strategy on the technology side, but failed to integrate it throughout the company and make staff aware of its plans and give them appropriate training. Feeling curious, we checked out this organization to see if the problem existed elsewhere. It became apparent to us that the same lack of understanding of the Web-based system existed among staff at all levels and in a wide variety of departments: reservation agents on the 800-number system, ticket agents in the airport, and staff at the gates.

E-biz projects, regardless of their purpose, have a wide-ranging impact on people throughout an organization. Everyone needs full and complete understanding of what the company is doing, why it is doing it, and why they should support the initiative. Developing staff understanding and buy-in to a corporate e-biz initiative is no small matter, especially because the people in many organizations may be wary of e-biz. If they are suspicious and their fears are not dispelled, they won't support the efforts of the company. And their lack of support will come out in confusing messages to the customer, and through customer service and interaction problems.

We are often called in to assist company management in helping sales and other staff understand the critical goals and importance of an e-biz strategy, and often witness this suspicion firsthand. Here's a good example of the nature of the challenge: We were brought into one company to help sales staff understand why the company was pushing so hard to have customers use an electronic ordering system. The e-biz strategy was extremely valid — the company's goal was to have 50 percent of corporate customer orders driven through its Web site. By doing so, it would shave a significant amount off the cost of day-to-day, routine orders. But there was another reason why it wanted the Web site to become a key part of the ordering process: If customers managed routine orders on their own, the sales staff would be freed up to spend their time more usefully with the customer.

The sales staff viewed the matter differently. Many of them believed that the purpose of the online ordering project was to put them out of a job. Their thinking was, "If our customers are buying through the Web site, I won't be needed." Many of them failed to see that the real goal of the project was to free up their time so they could do what they do best — working with the customers in an advisory capacity, in order to encourage them to buy more!

The result was that, from the point of view of the customers, the organization and its sales staff were often working at cross-purposes. The company was busy promoting its e-commerce procurement initiative, while sales staff were trying not to promote it, or dismissing it if customers asked about it. All kinds of suspicion will arise when tinkering is done to improve the customer-support process. This response is common, and another reason why organizations need to work hard to ensure that all staff understand why they are doing what they are doing.

Lack of Internal Coordination

When it comes to e-biz, organizations have to work harder to coordinate their e-biz activities with the different groups who are affected by the strategy, or who are involved in making sure that components of the strategy work properly. A key point is that every individual and every department within a company are going to be affected by e-biz. No one is immune.

This flies in the face of many organizational cultures. In the past, some staff and executives had the attitude that people only needed to know how to do their own job, not how their job affected other departments or how they might be affected by the activities of other groups. But, for e-biz to be successful, companies have to accept that employees need a general understanding of how all the operations work. After all, there are many pieces to the e-biz puzzle, and a company has to ensure that someone takes responsibility for getting all the pieces of the puzzle to fit together.

PROBLEMS WITH CUSTOMER SERVICE

- Eighty-seven percent of companies fail to provide "adequate" responses to e-mail questions.

- Thirty-eight percent of companies have no e-mail support infrastructure in place.

- Forty-six percent of the highest-traffic sites take five days or more to respond to e-mail.

- Only eight percent of the 69,500 call centres in the U.S. include Web support.

- E-mail autoresponses sent to respond to customer queries are wrong 30 to 50 percent of the time.

Source: *Telemarketing and Call Centre Solutions*, October 1, 2000

So many e-commerce initiatives go wrong because a tremendous amount of coordination is required within an organization to ensure that the myriad components of the e-biz strategy are put in place. Often no one will take on the responsibility of ensuring that everything is done properly, with the result that the customer suffers.

Consider this: The airline that we previously mentioned added us to its list of most frequent flyers. Included in the list of benefits was a special e-mail address that could be used only by their most important customers. We sent a message to this special mailbox, only to have it rejected because the mailbox did not yet exist! Think about what that situation implied. One side of the house was busy implementing some type of Internet customer service, but either they didn't follow through or the individual/department responsible failed in their undertaking. These problems are related to poor human resources coordination. The staff in various departments should have been educated about the new systems — before they were advertised to customers.

Lack of Integrated Customer-Contact Systems

Another area where companies are failing at customer support is in the lack of integration of their databases, e-mail systems, call centres, and other technology systems used for customer support. Coordinating technological strategies is a complex undertaking. One example of the need for integrated systems is the customer who chooses to contact the organization in a variety of different ways. One day the customer will phone in a query to a retail salesperson, the next day he'll send an e-mail message, and the following day he might send a fax to the service department. He expects all of his concerns to be bundled together.

But most companies haven't invested in technology that will let them integrate all their customer databases and contacts. So, the employee whom the customer is dealing with will not have a history of the interactions that customer has had with the organization by telephone, e-mail, or other methods. The customer then becomes frustrated by having to repeat information, and feels the company has failed at customer service.

One of the most popular and significant corporate initiatives in the field of customer service today involves "customer relationship management" (CRM) systems, which are designed to give a company a "360-degree view" of all interactions with its customers. In other words, these systems let someone see the entire history of the interactions that every customer has had with the company.

COMPANIES MUST MAKE CHOICES

As the issues raised above show, becoming a customer-centred organization is a challenging task.

Of course, another perspective on the empowered consumer suggests that consumers' demands for a one-hour response time to an e-mail question might be unreasonable, and that their quality-of-service expectations might also be too high. It simply may not be possible for companies to respond that fast, goes this line of thinking. Perhaps there should be an upper limit on what companies can reasonably and profitably be expected to deliver. Perhaps, over time, if everyone is unable to respond to consumer demands, then their expectations of support will be reduced.

Certainly, if it is not profitable for companies to gear up their support operations to respond to e-mails within one hour, they won't do it. We've seen this type of imbalance between the need for profit and customer expectations with the Internet before. Many online retail companies started offering free shipping because customers were demanding it — it became a competitive necessity to offer free shipping. But now most online retailers have stopped offering this service because it's unprofitable to do so. Could this situation repeat itself with other aspects of customer demand and service requirements generated by the Internet? Perhaps.

But we also believe that the Internet leads to massive competition in almost every sector, so one of the few distinguishing factors among so many different companies will be excellence of customer service. Companies must choose how to allocate their resources, and those that neglect the customer service area may eventually find that their decision has a depressing effect on the bottom line.

Some companies are choosing to offer excellent customer service only to their most important clients, while delivering automatic, canned responses or support to infrequent customers. Fidelity Investments led the way in the U.S. by doing this, and quickly gained the attention of the business sector. Taking a long-term view, however, we expect that there will be a steady, ongoing increase in the quality of customer service in order to meet customer expectations. Service failures, after all, are occurring in an environment that is very dangerous for companies. The Internet is bringing about a subtle but distinct shift in the relationship between businesses and their customers. Not only is comparison shopping becoming easier, thanks to the Web, but customers are becoming empowered in other ways. The best way to put this into perspective is through an example.

A number of years ago, one of the authors had a major home renovation done. Not surprisingly, his house features an alarm system. Given the size of the renovation, we asked a local alarm company to come in and give us an idea about what would be involved in extending the system to all the new doors and windows. (This company was the one that did the original installation.) Within only a few minutes, the representative suggested that a new alarm box would be required, since the current one would not be able to support the increased number of doors and windows. The cost would be around $1,800.

After the representative left, we took a look at the existing alarm box, found the name of the manufacturer, and hit the Web. In a matter of moments, we had found the company and located our particular alarm box. It took only a few moments more to determine that the problem could be solved by adding an accessory circuit card, for a price of around $200. We quickly sent an e-mail message to the manufacturer and received a response within a day, confirming that this was a workable solution. At that point, we politely called the local alarm company, indicated we wanted the $200 solution, and suggested that in the future they should have a better understanding of the products they purport to represent, or be more honest in their recommendations.

What does this situation imply? That organizations today must struggle with the fact that customers can quickly and effectively examine their purchasing or service options and come to their own conclusions as to what they should be doing. The Internet has had a massive impact on the sales process. This experience showed us that not only are companies challenged by ensuring their staff understand the role of the Internet in the customer relationship, they also need to make sure that their distribution-channel partners are on side. Companies that represent the products or services of other organizations need to take the time to ensure that their sales representatives fully understand and support the e-commerce/e-biz efforts of their suppliers. Once again, integration of e-business strategy is key — which isn't necessarily easy, as we will see.

ELEMENTS OF GOOD ONLINE CUSTOMER CARE

At first glance, it might seem a straightforward process to create an effective online customer-care centre and provide for online interaction. Many organizations might think that they have done so. After all, they've put up a Web site, listed an e-mail address, allowed a few account inquiries, and written a "Frequently Asked Questions" page. We beg to differ. We believe that these organizations have barely scratched the surface in terms of utilizing the Internet as an effective customer-support tool. A lot of effort will have to go towards building and maintaining sophisticated, all-encompassing customer-support sites, regardless of the size of the company. Effective online customer support calls for the following elements:

- **E-mail response management:** provides effective customer support through a system that deals efficiently with incoming e-mail questions and provides a timely response. Customers demand to be able to send in a message and get a quick reply.

- **Customer information centre:** allows for customer self-service. Customers, whether they are consumers or other business organizations, now expect to access a full range of useful information relevant to their needs. This means not just marketing literature, but everything that might help them with a problem, including manuals, summaries of frequently asked questions (FAQs), technical documents, and other information that seeks to address issues or questions that customers may have.

- **Integrated customer-contact systems:** allow employees to give excellent service and have access to all of a customer's information, regardless of how the contact was made — by phone, fax, e-mail, etc. This is a huge area of effort, one that generally falls within the scope of customer relationship management (CRM), an issue that has become a multibillion-dollar industry.

- **Customer interaction:** allows customers to instantly access order status, transaction details, and other historical information related to their business relationship. Hence, the extension of accounting and transaction systems described in the previous chapter is a key part of the new customer relationship.

All of the above should be implemented in a way that helps to personalize interactions and encourage and build customer loyalty in order to create repeat customers. In the new era of e-biz, it is inevitable that if a company undertakes to satisfy the support and interaction demands of its customers, it is going to try to leverage that investment in order to increase sales.

Let's look at the first three elements in a little more detail.

E-mail Response Management

One of the biggest areas of opportunity is going to emerge with sophisticated, large-scale projects that aim to deal with the e-mail support problem. It is an important step for an organization to fully accept the role and importance of Internet support. It should be prepared to post detailed contact information on its Web site, but doing so isn't useful unless the organization is prepared to follow up quickly when contact is made.

In the past several years this is quite clearly an area that most organizations have failed at — miserably. Yet that isn't surprising. Imagine the problems that a company with a Web site faces. To provide Internet-based customer support, they must publish an e-mail address (or a series of e-mail addresses) on their support pages, as well as elsewhere throughout their site. But once they do so, they are flooded with questions from customers. They may have been in business for many years, providing support via an 800 number and traditional methods, but they have never before encountered the massive numbers of messages descending upon them like locusts.

They simply don't have an infrastructure that can deal with these messages. There is no system by which to tag and track each e-mail so that its status can be determined, nor is there a method to route specific messages to specific departments or people so they can be adequately followed up. Indeed, there are probably no systems at all in place to deal with these queries! This means that, inevitably, messages are not answered — or worse, are lost forever — with the result that customers become infuriated.

Consider the experience of SunTrust, one of the top ten U.S. banks. Three years ago, they could count on one hand the number of e-mail messages they got per day. Of course, the company expected to see an increase in e-mail after it merged with another bank in mid-2000. But soon they were receiving 30,000 messages a month, and had to dedicate 20 people to the job of answering e-mail.

> According to research firm IDC Canada, the number of worldwide e-mail messages sent on an average day will grow to 18 billion in 2003 from five billion in 1999. Approximately 25 per cent of all customer contact will occur on-line, spawning a huge demand for e-mail repliers.
>
> "New E-slaves," *Globe and Mail*, April 3, 2000

As discussed earlier, this e-mail blizzard is happening in a world where customer-support expectations are extremely high. After all, how many times have you heard people complain that they sent a question to a company via their Web site and never heard back from them? The statistics bear this out: Report after report indicates that more than 50 percent of major companies still don't answer e-mail messages within a reasonable period of time.

This is a dangerous situation that businesses find themselves in. In this era of heightened competition, there is no doubt that people are far more likely to take their business elsewhere if they feel they aren't getting an adequate response from a company they are dealing with. E-mail failure is a critical fault line in the new relationship between a company and its customers. And so failure with e-mail support can have an extremely adverse effect on the bottom line. Providing quick answers to customer questions that come through the Web site is critical to any future success with that customer.

> E-mail customer contacts are expected to grow by more than 250 percent between 1998 and 2001. In some industries, more than 80 percent of customer contacts will be through e-mail or Web-based forms by 2001.
>
> Source: Forrester Research and Gartner Group, 1999

Companies have to invest heavily to ensure that they are doing the right things. Quite a few people were stunned when they learned that at one time Chapters, the Canadian bookseller, was employing upwards of 65 people simply to handle e-mail questions. It was their job to deal with the 4,000 daily e-mail messages that the company was receiving and to respond to most messages within two hours.

When you consider the scope of the Chapters effort, you realize the complexity of the situation. Coping with the mass of e-mail messages a company receives means ensuring that

- customer-support questions are routed to the appropriate people within the organization;
- the status of questions in the queue is somehow monitored so that backlogs are cleared appropriately;
- customers are notified that their questions have been received and are assigned a tracking number with which they can follow up;
- details on the status of questions by a specific customer can be ascertained quickly and linked or referenced to other information the company has about the customer, such as order or payment history;
- answers previously provided can be reused in order to avoid wasting support-staff resources in reinventing the wheel: typing out the same answer over and over again and spending time recreating information that already exists;
- issues being raised in e-mail queries are monitored so that new information can be placed on the Web site as appropriate or other corrective action can be undertaken.

That's a lot of stuff that needs to be taken care of — for what might seem to be a rather simple business issue.

How big a problem is customer e-mail support? Let's put it into perspective in light of the experience of Amazon.com. A *Calgary Herald* article noted that "customer service representatives are expected to maintain a high rate of productivity, and output is watched closely, several employees said. A stellar Amazon representative can respond to 12 e-mails in an hour; lagging productivity — fewer than 7.5 e-mails an hour for an extended period — can result in probation or termination" ("Amazon.Calm," January 22, 2000).

Put that rate of productivity up against the previously mentioned Harris Poll study that suggested that in 2001 people will be sending some 50 million e-mail questions a day. Assuming that in a typical eight-hour shift a person could deal with almost a hundred e-mail questions, this implies that in the "new economy" there might be upwards of half a million people worldwide needed to answer e-mail. No wonder so many companies don't answer e-mail on a timely basis!

It is for these reasons that we are seeing such growth in software to help cope with the e-mail deluge, and increasing numbers of projects to implement smoothly functioning e-mail support systems. Let's make things even more complicated: A company might encounter, because of a current promotion or some other issue, a massive spike in the number of e-mail questions that it receives. It has to be able to ramp up its capability quickly to deal with such increases in the need for customer support. How does it acquire the ability to deal with a sudden influx of customer-support queries? Understand this, and you'll realize that an e-mail support system can suddenly become a huge undertaking — and a pretty big opportunity.

A growing number of companies are putting together the sophisticated e-mail management software that organizations will need to manage the deluge. Study some of their sites and you will get a sense of the software and solutions that are becoming available. (Some of these organizations have multiple customer-support products that cover many different aspects, so make sure you home in on the e-mail support solutions.)

E.piphany	www.epiphany.com
Kana Communications Inc.	www.kana.com
Clarify (owned by Nortel)	www.clarify.com
Siebel Systems	www.siebel.com
EGain Communications	www.egain.com

Customer Information Centres

Another key aspect of a customer-centred organization is that it builds and maintains an effective customer-care area within its Internet initiative. There can be many different aspects to such an information centre, depending on the industry the company is in and what its customers (whether they are individuals or businesses) require, and depending on how far down the path it decides to go. We see opportunities in three areas: the dynamic FAQ, content management, and corporate knowledge.

The Dynamic FAQ

A well-known rule of thumb states that 80 percent of customers' problems can be solved with just 20 percent of the available information on a Web site. This is why so many organizations work into their sites the concept of the FAQ, or summary of frequently asked questions. The goal of such a document is to provide customers with the most likely answers to problems they may have.

> **Seventy-eight percent of consumers check for a "Frequently Asked Questions" summary before contacting a company with a question.**
>
> Source: *Telemarketing and Call Centre Solutions*, October 1, 2000

Most organizations have some form of basic FAQ document. FAQs are, after all, static documents — a company figures out the commonly asked questions, puts together a list of answers, and hopes that this will ward off lots of customer contact. For example, consider the FAQ at Royal Bank. It provides a number of answers to common questions about buying a car:

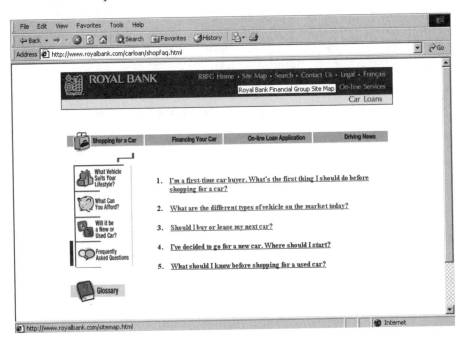

But such a document can't deal with the fact that questions from customers will constantly evolve. For example, say the bank launches a new type of car loan, or competitors offer a new type of loan that is somewhat controversial. A variety of new questions might come in from customers. Support staff at the bank would then seek clarification about the official policy and response of the bank, or might direct particular staff to help customers assess their loan options. Over time, the situation might lead to a series of new FAQs — and answers. In an ideal world, a company would track all the new questions, determine which were the most popular, and accumulate the answers so it would not be reinventing the wheel over and over again.

Some organizations are moving beyond the simple FAQ document; they realize that answers provided to e-mail questions are a powerful source of knowledge. We are seeing the emergence of software that allows these answers to be built into a database that is accessible online to other customers. We might call these "dynamic FAQs." Polaroid is one organization that is taking advantage of this emerging capability.

"The FAQ has cut down dramatically on the number of e-mails to our customer call centres," Cohen says. Polaroid began using the RightNow software for Web FAQs on a hosted basis last winter. Since then, customer contact reports show that customer e-mail volume has dropped by about one-third, while the number of visitors each month to Polaroid.com has roughly doubled to 50,000.

"CALL CENTRES FEELING WEB'S IMPACT: CUSTOMER RELATIONSHIP MANAGEMENT
SOFTWARE GETS A BOOST FROM WEB FAQS, CHAT AND OTHER TOOLS,"
NETWORK WORLD, AUGUST 21, 2000

A leader in this area is RightNow (www.rightnow.com), which is helping companies accumulate information and establish dynamic FAQs. These extensive resources, accessible within a Web site, go many steps further in helping customers obtain answers to their questions. The RightNow Web software allows companies to feed into a database the many e-mail questions received and the answers that are generated. It allows the customer to search the database in a variety of ways, by key word, phrase, category, or subcategory. Many companies are using the RightNow software, including Air Canada (www.aircanada.com), Ben and Jerry's (www.benjerry.com), McKesson Chemical (www.mckhboc.com), and Schwinn Cycling (www.schwinn.com).

Take a look at the FAQs at these sites, and you'll get an idea of the sophistication of this type of application. (You'll also get a sense of the number of e-mail support questions that such companies get!) At the Ben and Jerry's site you can search for a particular word, pick a particular category, or sort your answer in a variety of ways.

Each question is given a reference number and tells you when it was created and the last time it was updated. The answers to the questions are generated from previously answered questions, so the company is combining the power of an FAQ with the knowledge it has gathered through its e-mail support system.

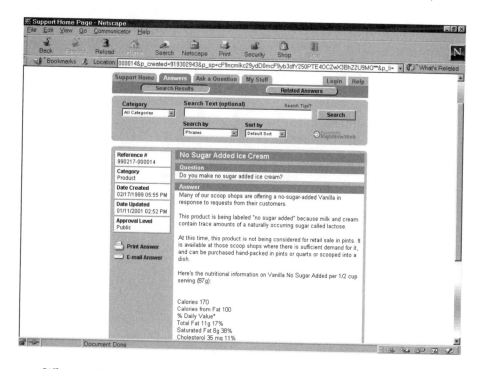

What are the benefits of such an approach? A cost-avoidance process is at work here. If a company effectively deploys a basic-level self-service section within its site, it can reduce the costs of other support mechanisms. The following information, from the RightNow Web site, gives you a hint as to the extent of these potential savings:

- Turner Broadcasting reduced the volume of e-mail to its general support mailbox by 75 percent by placing online a series of carefully determined questions.

- By using the RightNow software to analyze questions, Ben & Jerry's was able to clear a backlog of 5,000 messages — reducing it by two-thirds — by placing 12 carefully selected answers to common questions online.

- PictureTel estimates that, given the sophisticated nature of its product, it cost about $60 to handle each inbound phone call. With its RightNow system, it reduced call volume by two-thirds, achieving significant savings.

- Sanyo reduced incoming service calls by 30 percent within 40 days of putting up a RightNow self-service section in its Web site.

- Air Canada saw a 60 percent reduction in e-mail once it had established its dynamic FAQ.

Note that results such as these might be questioned; after all, these numbers come from the company trying to sell the product being discussed. But if the results are to be believed, they demonstrate the big benefits of using software that helps you constantly analyze the customer-support queries coming in, and respond accordingly. There are other companies similar to RightNow, such as Answers.com. In addition, other customer-support tools that we discuss in this chapter usually have some element that allows the integration of e-mail queries and answers into a database, either online or accessible only by staff.

Content Management

Customers demand all kinds of information from their support experience. They believe that company Web sites should make readily available to them a wide variety of information sources, including searchable document databases, technical documents and manuals, product summaries, problem-solving guides, and anything else that can help them in their particular situation. As the Internet becomes more a part of their lives, they will increasingly use the quality and depth of information available online to decide whom to do business with.

Once again, customer expectations are being set by organizations at the leading edge. Anyone who has sought technical information or assistance from computer and other high-tech companies is familiar with how those organizations are providing very effective customer support. Take a look at 3Com, for example, and you will find several elements integrated into their Web site, which is easy to use and very comprehensive.

From the main page, you can choose a specific product category or an area you are interested in (for example, Home & Home Office). Here we have chosen to find out about home networking products:

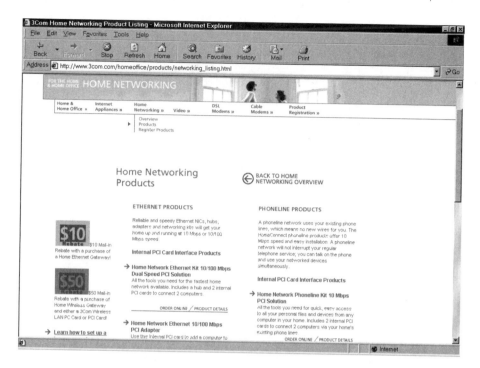

Eventually we can find out the product's price, its features and benefits, detailed specifications, and even warranty information:

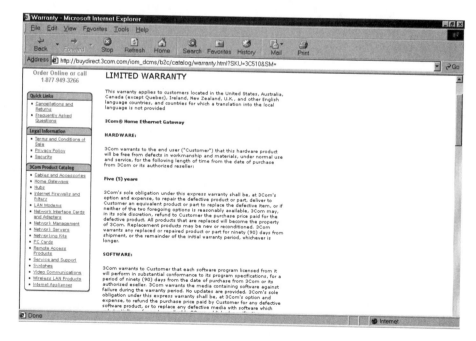

If you need software for the product you have ordered, you can get it from their software library:

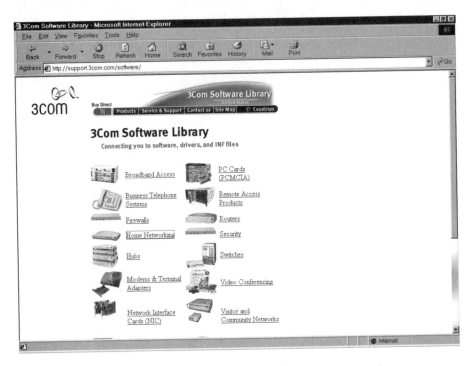

Not only that, but we can hit the 3Com Knowledgebase, which is a database of information to help you solve your installation, configuration, and upgrade problems:

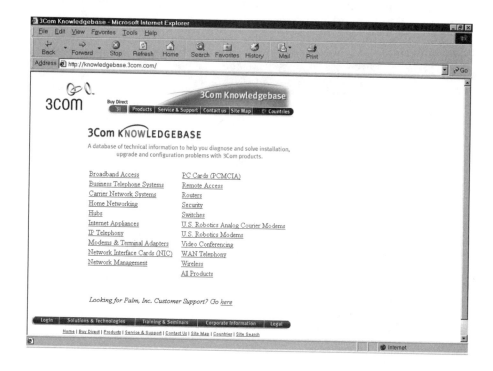

3Com provides an example of the excellence found in many high-tech company Web sites, and which will become necessary for most other organizations. It is comprehensive and combines marketing information with technical support, product literature, manuals, and other information. And after customers have used a site such as this, they begin to think they should get similar service everywhere else.

As noted before, an example of an organization that is setting the pace for government groups is the Government of North Carolina (www.ncgov.com), which has a renowned "e-government" strategy. Spend some time browsing this site, and you'll get a sense of where governments will need to go.

Whether you are a citizen, a business, or a state employee, you will be able to find what you are looking for in this massive site. It is meant to answer questions, not to explain government hierarchies (the focus of so many other government sites), and is designed with the "customer/constituent" in mind.

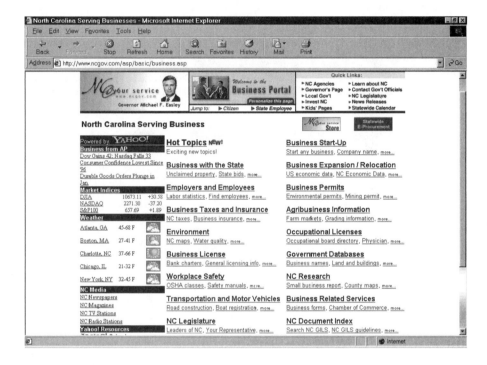

Finally, from a business-to-business perspective, check out the sophistication of what GE Plastics is doing. Browse through the site, and you will discover that all of GE's business units are very good when it comes to support information. Pick one — say, the GE Silicones site. You could spend hours in here exploring an extremely sophisticated, business-oriented customer-support site.

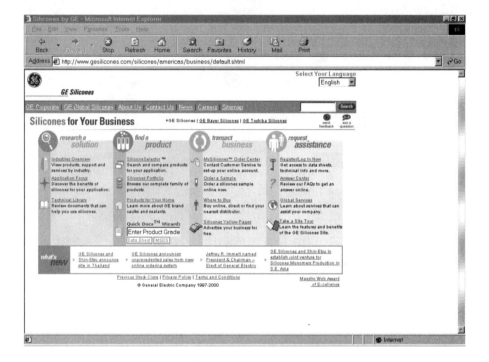

For example, examine the support section of this site, and you will see that they are providing as much self-service information as possible:

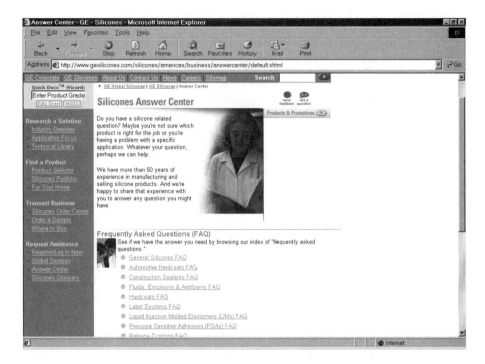

These sites will give you a sense of the sophistication required to support client relationships. The key strategy driving these efforts, aside from providing excellent customer service, is to drive down costs. Sophisticated customer support in this regard certainly makes sense.

Think about the effort that has gone into creating such sites as those demonstrated above. Clearly, the undertaking is massive, given the volumes of information involved. This emerging area of the Internet has come to be called "content management."

Simply expressed, as customers demand more information, Web sites find themselves wrestling with a heck of a lot more content. In the early days of the Web, it was a fairly straightforward process — put up a Web site, add a few pages of information, and you were done with it. But now, with some Web sites swelling to tens of thousands of pages, it is no longer an easy process for any organization, large or small. The information management problem became much worse when organizations suddenly realized that they had several different Web sites serving many different audiences and objectives. Add to that the fact that, as companies work to serve a global audience, they often have to provide Web services in several languages.

Think about the challenges the organizations above faced in order to manage their support infrastructure:

- The company has to ensure that all information is current and up-to-date, and that stale information is removed from the site on a regular basis. It must do this to avoid problems with customers, but there is another, critical reason why an organization must carefully manage information on its site. If a site contains promotion information on a sale that is no longer in effect, the company could find itself charged with false or misleading advertising.

- There must be a process of internal coordination among various departments to ensure that new information generated throughout the organization is fed into the "Web system." This includes new marketing material, technical manuals, and other information.

- Ideally, there should be some capability of establishing a "feedback loop," similar to what might have been done with e-mail, to determine which specific problems, documents, or issues are being targeted in the customer-care centre.

- The company must ensure that only information that should be available online is placed online. Security of information is a major concern, and organizations need to consider the types of permission they will require for access to particular documents.

- Procedures must be in place to convert information from other sources or production streams over to a format suitable for the Web. In the case of a catalogue operation, this could involve tens of thousands of pictures.

- The company must figure out methods of organizing the data so that customers, suppliers, or business partners can easily find the information they are looking for.

- Strategies must take into account an environment of constantly changing information and the inevitable need to expand the Web site. It is estimated that some Web sites double or triple in size every six months.

It is for reasons like these that content management software has gained such prominence over the last several years, with the establishment of companies like Documentum, ePrise, FileNet, Interwoven, OpenMarket, Broadvision, and others. Hit the sites of these organizations, study what they offer, and you will discover a whole new area of opportunity that you might not have realized existed.

There are many differences between these organizations and the nature of the solutions that they offer, to such a degree that information technology journals spend a great deal of time explaining the differences. Some were originally designed to assist organizations in managing documents and were then subsequently adapted to the Web, while others were designed specifically to help organizations manage their Web content. But the difference in approaches is not what is important here. During the next 20 years, organizations are going to be spending a significant amount of time and money learning how to get the information they generate to fit better into the customer-centric business model.

That is where you might discover opportunity, since the area can be one of significant complexity. Consider some of the elements of the software mentioned above:

- personalization
- workflow
- links to other systems
- ease of use

The entire process by which an organization turns its face outwards via the Web is going to provide plenty of opportunity for those who choose to get involved.

Corporate Knowledge

The central activity of a knowledge creating company is to filter personal knowledge and translate that into corporate knowledge. For which the first step is to change corporate culture.

"KM IS READY FOR TAKE OFF," *ECONOMIC TIMES,* FEBRUARY 8, 2001

Carried to its logical conclusion, the customer-support dilemma is helping to force organizations to wrestle with the issue of what to do with their overall corporate knowledge. Herein lies a key point — the Internet and e-biz are forcing a significant shift in the way that organizations think about information. They have helped many companies understand that they have done a poor job of harnessing their collective corporate knowledge.

When dealing with customer support through e-mail and the Web and wrestling with content management issues, companies have come to realize that a tremendous amount of important organizational information is generally unavailable. Yes, organizations have been generating reports and documents and manuals and other information, but few efforts have been made to archive such corporate information so that it is available within the company on a widespread basis, not to mention accessible to customers when necessary.

Suddenly, aggressive consumers have become far more demanding than ever before, and are looking for instantaneous response to their questions. In terms of information resources, companies simply aren't in good enough shape to provide them with what they want. That's why the concept of "corporate knowledge" has come into vogue during the past ten years; the arrival of the Internet has intensified attention to this issue. Companies now understand the value of corporate knowledge and believe that it must be captured and made available for both internal and external purposes, because they realize that, day by day, an important asset is being lost. They have slowly come to recognize that the knowledge being generated by staff represents a powerful asset, and that often the value of that asset is being squandered or irrevocably lost.

Consider the problems.

First, within most companies, few systems are designed to capture what staff know. People work on a day-to-day basis, often within a paper environment, accumulating lots of special information about a wide variety of issues, many of which might relate to questions asked by customers via the Internet. None of that information is "captured" by a system that would permit other staff to access it.

Second, few systems even attempt to organize, let alone document and inventory, the different customer-related systems. Most companies work in what we might call "information silos" — everybody does their own thing, often with little regard to the activities and information generated by other departments. Marketing departments create their promotional literature, product developers write manuals, quality-control staff document the results of their tests, manufacturing staff document the production process, and sales staff have their own resources related to the product, not to mention a dozen or so other departments that might also generate information.

Third, all of this information exists in splendid isolation. The company has no idea what exists, who has prepared it, how useful it might be, or how to access it. It comes in a wide variety of formats, both paper and electronic. Some information might be kept by individual staff members, some might be held by departments, and a tiny amount might be available on an organization-wide basis.

The knowledge management challenge is made worse because the culture of organizations doesn't often encourage accumulation and sharing of important information. Many companies have a power structure in which information has strategic value. This creates a culture in which people accumulate information and then jealously guard access to it, acting out the old maxim "Knowledge is power."

Finally, to make things worse, important and useful knowledge often walks out the door when staff members depart the organization. Not coordinating the accumulation of corporate knowledge has a dreadful impact on customer support. Identical queries are researched and answered again and again, leading to massive duplication of effort and waste of resources.

So there is a lot of information about, but since none of it is readily accessible to anyone who might need it, it is often "lost" just as soon as it is generated. The result? Most companies are gigantic "knowledge drains" in which valuable information is repeatedly generated and then lost.

A study by Delphi Communications, a major player in the knowledge-management industry, estimates that almost half of corporate knowledge exists within the brains of staff — where it is virtually inaccessible, on a routine and straightforward basis, to much of the organization.

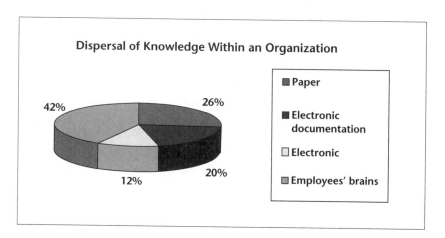

What are the benefits if companies manage to harness corporate information? They are manifold — indeed, it is expected that this will be one of the keys to future success, and perhaps even survival. And there is a definite customer-support element.

The scope of the projects that will unfold in this area is enormous. Customer support and CRM projects are only one small aspect of corporate knowledge projects, but their growing importance has helped make the project of capturing and harnessing corporate knowledge one of the most important areas of focus in information technology today. It is estimated that the knowledge-management software market grew from a mere $48 million (U.S.) in 1996 to some $390 million in 1999 — just a hint as to its growth!

Throughout the corporate sector, massive efforts are being made, and will continue to be made, to grab the collective knowledge of employees so the information can be used for a variety of purposes, one of which is as a source of information for Web queries. Don't delude yourself about the size and scale of such an endeavour — it looks to be something of a Manhattan Project for every company, or perhaps less a project than a mindset. Companies first have to get into the frame of mind in which they recognize the importance of harvesting internal knowledge. They then have to figure out the many different ways to do that over time. Thus we have seen the appearance of executives known as "chief knowledge officers," who can steer companies through the long, complicated voyage into a culture in which knowledge is captured and used.

What can we suggest here? As you study and examine your options, always keep in mind that the buzz-phrase "corporate knowledge" is like an iceberg — we can see a little of it above the surface, but there promises to be much more below. We think this area will take on increasing importance for every organization, well into the future.

Integrated Customer-Contact Systems

As we mentioned above, an integrated customer-contact system gives employees access to all the information about a customer, regardless of how he or she contacted the company. Such a system is often called customer relationship management, or CRM.

What is CRM? A good way to describe it is as a business application, the primary goal of which is to use information technology to learn more about your customers and their activities, whims, and buying patterns, in order to provide them with better service and to enhance your sales opportunities. A good CRM strategy could be used to target specific customers with a promotion. It could be used prior to a sales call to let sales staff examine not only the complete sales history and results of sales calls for a particular customer, but also other interactions or details. It would allow a support person to see the entire history of the company's interaction with the customer, including previous complaints or other issues. This "360-degree view of the customer" approach has rightly caught fire in the business world.

The issue of CRM is beyond the scope of this book. However, you should be aware that many CRM initiatives and programs are being modified so that Internet customer support is part of what they address, and they themselves are becoming tightly integrated with the Internet.

A CULTURE OF E-SUPPORT

Finally, we come to a point that we think is extremely important. The era of e-biz is going to force companies to develop what we might call a culture of e-support. Real e-biz support is something more than e-mail, information repositories, and online interaction. To really succeed with customer support, a company must truly believe that excellence in customer service, both online and offline, is of paramount importance.

Business has a long way to go in this regard; few companies seem to be doing what is necessary to make such a cultural shift. By failing so miserably online, many have demonstrated that, to them, excellence in customer support is not an important issue. The business press has been full of such stories, which indicates that many Canadian organizations don't seem to measure up when it comes to support issues — whether the support is offered though an in-store experience, an 800 number, or some other route.

But the era of the Internet and e-biz changes all of this. As we have indicated, the new consumers are extremely unforgiving when it comes to poor customer service, and they now have the option of quickly taking their business elsewhere. Companies that don't respond will discover that their lack of a support culture is harming them.

The bottom line? We believe that the Internet is resulting in such heightened expectations that every organization is going to have to become customer-centric — that is, to develop a culture in which the very mission of the organization is to excel at dealing with the customer. And that, more than anything, indicates that this is a field where there will be unprecedented opportunity in the years to come.

Part III

Career Opportunities and Issues

Chapter 6

Thinking About Where the Jobs Are

> *One of the things people will have to learn is that they will have to take charge of their own career.* PETER DRUCKER

> *This industry is not about technology, it's about business — many people misunderstand that.* EMAD RIZKALLA, ZEDDCOMM

THE QUESTION FOR YOU NOW BECOMES, "HOW CAN I DISCOVER emerging opportunities as the world of e-biz unfolds?" First, you should take some time to get a sense of both the threats and the opportunities that might arise from the issues identified in the previous chapters. Do this in a rather broad frame of mind, in terms of the big picture of how jobs and careers are going to change.

In order to help you with this task, we outline what we believe will be some of the major issues people will face when it comes to e-biz and its impact on their jobs and careers in the future.

- **There will be plenty of new opportunity, but also less job and career security.** In the previous chapters, we outlined some of the fundamental areas where companies and government organizations will concentrate their e-biz activities during the next several years, or how they might be affected by e-biz. That discussion will help you understand that there is a lot of work to be done as the corporate and government sectors streamline their operations with the Internet, and as they learn to use the Internet to deal with clients in new ways. As the Internet continues to give companies opportunities to pursue new business models and new ways of doing business, there is no doubt that there will also be new career and job opportunities within those organizations.

But with every opportunity comes a threat, and the fact remains that the Internet and e-biz will present a significant challenge to many jobs and careers. We believe that, over the long term, we will see a good deal of turmoil within the corporate and government sectors as the changes that we outline in these chapters begin to take hold. Why? Because the end result of e-biz will be, as we indicate, that there are going to be many changes in the way that business is conducted and in the way that it "works." Many jobs will be subject to change. You would be deluding yourself to think that the way you work today will be the same as the way you will work in the connected economy of tomorrow.

That is why you should keep your mind open to both the opportunity and the threat — the Internet and e-biz are a double-edged sword. Examine the issues we've identified in light of how they could represent an opportunity to discover a new job or career. But at the same time, think about what we have said, in order to assess whether you have what it takes to survive any threats that the Internet and e-biz might represent.

- **Your skills may not be as relevant or as useful as they were.** Another sad reality is that you might not have the skills required by your employer as the organization prepares to cope with the e-business age. A study undertaken by the recruiting firm Towers Perrin in 2000 suggested that many executives don't believe their staff possess the necessary skills to cope with e-biz. (The study was based on interviews with executives of large multinational companies, most of them in Canada, the United States, and Britain.)

   Towers Perrin found that 87 percent of the companies surveyed think their managers lack the skills and capabilities needed to deal with e-commerce. What's more, 66 percent admit they have trouble attracting qualified people to deal with e-business. Opinions like these help explain the much-hyped "skills shortage" so often talked about in the press. They also imply that, at the early stage of e-biz implementation, companies found that many of their staff were barely up to dealing with the issue. Hence, they relied a great deal on external consultants to assist with e-biz strategy and implementation.

   Will this state of affairs continue? We think so. Many people will never be able to make the transition from a routine job to a strategic one. Why? Because their attitudes get in the way (more on that in a moment).

- **It's not all technical jobs and careers.** Okay, so you need to be motivated by the opportunity and ready to take on the challenge. What else do you need to think about?

  It is important that you don't fall into the trap of thinking that you can't discover opportunity in the high-tech economy because you don't have high-tech skills. We've found over the years that many people are convinced they don't have any skills that will be useful as the wired economy unfolds. Why? Because when they try to envision new opportunities with the Internet and e-biz, they put all the potential jobs into a great big box labelled "geek." They tend to think that, because they aren't computer geeks, they don't have any useful skills for the wired economy. Or worse, they simply decide that they don't want to do the type of work that geeks do!

  You may enjoy dealing with the technical side of things, but, as you have seen in this book so far, countless new opportunities are emerging with the Internet, many of them completely nontechnical in nature. And that perhaps represents one of the biggest secrets of the computer revolution: Most of the emerging jobs and careers don't deal directly with the technology — they are in other areas.

  As you consider your options, open your mind to the fact that many upcoming projects are going to have very little to do with technology. Instead, they will involve formulating business strategies, project planning, consulting, re-engineering business processes and procedures, training, managing, and still other areas. If you take the time to consider what we discussed about Internet myths, you will appreciate that the scope of e-biz efforts goes way beyond the technical to involve many different activities and skills.

- **Your attitude may get in the way.** Of course, to take advantage of the opportunities unfolding, you've got to be in the right frame of mind. And many people aren't.

  In an earlier chapter we indicated that one reason e-biz has been slow to take off is that people and organizations are highly resistant to change. When it comes to changing careers, resistance is probably at an all-time high. People don't like things that affect their jobs or careers — they tend to want things to stay the way they are. But e-biz is going to cause significant change.

That is why attitude has a definite impact on your potential for success in the unfolding world of e-biz. Lots of people won't be able to cope with the changes that the world of e-biz represents; indeed, they will be pushed out the door if they can't handle new ways of doing business. If your frame of mind won't let you accept the changes that will occur, or if you fight them — knowingly or subconsciously — you'll enjoy less success. That is a basic fact, since much of what is going to happen with e-biz is inevitable, whether you like it or not.

We have taken some criticism in the past for the blunt way in which we express this reality. Some reviewers of our previous books have suggested we should be gentler in the manner we use to encourage people to adapt to the Internet or e-biz, or that we should not use fear as a tool to motivate people to change. They have suggested that we be less aggressive in outlining the impact of the Internet on jobs and careers, or that we tone down our opinion that people might find themselves out of jobs because of their attitude towards change. To that we say, "Phooey!"

We believe that the business world is going to undergo some pretty gut-wrenching and dramatic change in the next 20 years, and that a lot of people are going to find themselves out of a job or with fewer opportunities because of their attitudes. People need to be scared! We don't think anyone can afford to be complacent about the scope and impact of the change that is going to happen. So we refuse to mince our words — the biggest barrier to your success could be your attitude.

The world of e-biz is one of constant exploration and testing of new ways of doing business, working, and sharing information. Such an environment requires an open mind, but we still regularly encounter people with attitudes that seem dead set — right from the get-go — against anything having to do with e-biz.

WHAT SHOULD YOU DO?

Here is a simple road map you can follow to find out what opportunities might be in front of you.

1. **Undertake a company and industry assessment.** Determine how you might be affected by what we have outlined in this book. For example, is your company in the midst of the kinds of initiatives or

projects described? What about the industry in which you work? If there isn't a lot happening, what will cause it to happen?

2. **Think about your possible role.** Is there an opportunity for you to get involved? What types of efforts are underway, and who is taking on various responsibilities? Is there a way that you can be proactive with potential projects in order to carve yourself out an opportunity? And if it is likely that your company won't be dealing with the areas and impacts of e-biz that we outline, are there other companies in your industry who are, that you might choose to get involved with instead?

3. **Undertake a skills self-assessment.** Take some time to think about your current skills and capabilities. Are they adequate for you to get involved with projects and initiatives involving e-biz? If not, are there any courses, workshops, or other forms of education that you might take to upgrade your skills? Do the vendors that supply your company with computer systems offer training and education? Are there ways in which you can get involved in various projects in order to gain practical experience?

4. **Assess your knowledge level.** Do you have enough knowledge to understand what we have described? Can you use some of the Web sites and issues we discuss to expand your knowledge beyond the confines of this book? How much do you know about how financial, transaction, manufacturing, or supply-chain systems might change within your organization? What are the major customer issues in your industry? What business models are being adopted? Who are the new and more challenging competitors? And what organizational changes already seem to be underway within your industry? Undertake an aggressive review of all these issues as they affect you, and you'll get a better sense of where the opportunities might be emerging.

Going through a process like this might help you establish your own, unique opportunities. Above all, keep an open mind. We are headed into uncharted territory with e-biz. We've provided you with a road map as far as we see it, but what you do with this road map is up to you. After all, it is you who are ultimately responsible for your future career and job opportunities.

WHAT DO THE EXPERTS SAY?

To help you get into the right frame of mind, we polled a broad cross-section of pioneers in the Canadian e-biz scene. We asked them for advice for people assessing opportunity in the wired economy, whether they are thinking of starting an Internet company, upgrading their skills to participate in e-commerce in their own companies, or planning to pursue a new career in the Internet/e-commerce industry.

Some of the executives and entrepreneurs we interviewed have been successful; others have not. Some have been active in the business-to-consumer space while others have been active in the business-to-business community. Whatever the case may be, many of our panel members have carried out intensive, large-scale Internet and e-biz projects, so we consider their insight and advice invaluable. (Full details on the participants can be found in the Appendix.)

Here's what we asked them: What piece of advice would you have for someone who's thinking of starting an Internet company, wants to change their career skills and capabilities to be a full participant in the e-commerce activities of their company, or is planning to change jobs so they can pursue a new career in the Internet/e-commerce industry?

Here's what they had to say:

Choose Your Opportunity Carefully

In light of the dot-com collapse, the wisdom of these pioneers is consistent — make sure that any choices you make about your job, opportunities, or career are sensible in light of the company you choose to get involved with. That much is a given.

PETER KRENKEL, NATURAL GAS EXCHANGE

This is a very exciting and glamorous area, but pick your opportunity carefully and be prepared for a multitude of changes. . . . The "easy money" investment has dried up and the early investors are now looking for signals that their money will generate returns. Try to avoid the "flavour of the month" and pick something that will have legs. How do you know? Good question. I generally look for opportunities that are simple yet "make sense"; i.e., if the business model is too complicated for you to understand, the customer probably won't understand it either. We all know that customers will not use things they do not understand.

It is interesting that many of them also suggest that you examine the values of the people you might become involved with, and assess your own values. Important advice, in light of the fact, as we've noted, that much of what went wrong with the Internet came about because greed took over.

SYED HASAN, RESPONSETEK NETWORKS
Do it if you relate to what the company is trying to bring to the marketplace and be sure you buy into the mechanism of operation (culture). Do not jump in for the gold rush and a big payoff. Also apply the same test to the most influential execs at the company — why are they doing it? For the love or money? If it is the latter, be aware that some of the decisions they make will not be for the whole company, but personal gain, and you may soon be standing on the wrong side of a merger/acquisition.

This issue of values is extremely important. In many cases, you will only succeed if you are driven by your passion for the task at hand, not for some imagined pot of gold at the end of the rainbow. In his observations, Peter Oxley of RewardStream perfectly captured the values that ruled the dot-com era, and the reason why they work against the success of so many people:

PETER OXLEY, REWARDSTREAM
My main piece of advice would be to look deep inside and understand your true motivations. I have encountered far too many Internet founders and early-stage employees that are dizzy with the prospect of attaining the staggering wealth that the New Economy is creating. They start each workday talking about the latest Internet stock prices, valuation, and future rounds of financing. This is the single largest distraction to the building of a successful and profitable company. Founders and new employees should pursue an Internet-based venture only if they are truly passionate about the business model. The combination of long hours and a hyperactive pace of decision making will eat an individual alive unless they are invigorated by the day-to-day business. All too often, the reality sets in that this is not the next Gold Rush. The latest downtick in the Internet stock market has really flushed out the motivations of many individuals in this space. . . . So if your reason for getting up in the morning is to prove to the world that your venture is the best thing since sliced bread, then join the Internet race. But remember, it's not a sprint — it's a marathon. And at every corner, an existing competitor or new entrant will be nipping at your heels.

Passion for the task at hand is critical to success. All of our panelists have worked long and hard to make their efforts succeed. Many of them indicated that what drives them is their belief that they are doing something worthwhile. Consider the comments from these folks:

SUHAYYA ABU-HAKIMA, AMIKANOW!
The biggest mistakes I have seen are based on the get-rich-quick mentality. Starting a wireless Internet company is very hard work and long hours. You do it because you are passionate about wanting to see a real-world problem solved, not because it is a quick way to get rich! You need to carefully build a very talented team, create an entrepreneurial culture, persevere, and stick to the old-fashioned idea of building up revenues based on solid business development. Most of all, you have to stay honest and ethical.

SCOTT RANKINE, METAMAIL
Above all else, go with something that excites you, something you can pour your heart and soul into. That's because, before you're finished, you will have mortgaged your life to make it happen, so you better have some fun doing it, or what's the point? Money is a poor yardstick by which to measure your personal worth — or anyone else's.

EMAD RIZKALLA, ZEDDCOMM
Do it because you like it, not because it is the place to be. Passion is a currency in the industry, and if you are not [passionate] about your concept or plan, you will not survive. This is probably one of the reasons this has been such a young person's game.

JULIE BRADSHAW, SUITE101.COM
Remember, excitement and passion are infectious. In my experience, people buy into people — so let your passion show!

Look for Solid Business Fundamentals

If you are assessing any type of e-biz or Internet opportunity and plan on making a career or job change to get involved, then avoid the mistake that so many fell into when dot-com dreams took over the economy. Jim Carroll wrote about this issue just as dot-com hysteria was reaching its peak ("Dot-com Careers Among Riskiest," *Globe and Mail*, February 21, 2000). In it, he noted:

Should you quit your job to join a dot-com? It's a question more and more people are asking themselves. It seems there is a massive exodus from the traditional business world to the universe of the dot-com.

Most recently, the business press has reported on the flood of professionals from leading U.S. law firms to the high-profile Silicon Valley Internet startups.

Certainly, the temptations spurring such moves are strong — particularly the stock options associated with dot-coms. These perks appear to be on an ever-increasing upward spiral, guaranteed to make you rich beyond your wildest dreams.

But it's not just the draw of the money that is gaining attention. Stuck in a humdrum job in a company that doesn't "get" the e-biz revolution, many people simply want to join the excitement of the dot-com universe, and become part of the work force that is out to change the world economy.

There's a party going on, and the natural inclination for people is to want to take part.

Yet most people pondering such a move also realize there is undeniable risk with any Internet organization. Unproven business models, spotty revenues, and uncertain guarantees regarding long-term survival make a dot-com career one of the riskiest around.

And, in what proved to be a prophetic statement, Jim observed:

Take the time to carefully research the organization that you join. There are a huge number of dot-coms out there, and some, quite simply, don't deserve to be in business, and probably won't be within a year.

The article prompted a flood of angry e-mail, complaining that he was ruining the party. Of course, shortly afterwards, the great dot-com shakeout began. Not surprisingly, our panel echoes our belief that you should make a very careful assessment of any type of Internet or e-biz activity you might become involved in.

BOB TAPSCOTT, MAPTUIT

What is the value proposition? Is this an intriguing new idea or something that has an actual income potential? Is this an idea that companies or individuals are willing to pay for? If the company does have a viable business proposition, does it have the alliances/capital required to have the message heard long enough to become profitable without massive dilution?

If so, can you participate in the value created? Internet companies are high-risk and, in rare cases, high-reward. If you are setting up a new Internet company, don't look initially for traditional venture capital. Look for customers that are willing to share in the risks and rewards that the Internet company offers.

JASON MANN, BRAINHUNTER.COM
If you are looking to join a firm, do your homework — find out what the funding situation is, what their burn rate is, how they plan to achieve their marketing objectives. Talk to employees already working at the firm. There is a strong tendency on the part of Internet companies (much like any company) to sell their firm in an interview, particularly in the competitive market conditions. It's important if you are making a career move to know that what you think you know about the firm is reality.

CHRIS COOK, GEARUNLIMITED.COM
Pick your industry/company wisely. Ensure they are fulfilling a real business need and that if the business plan were executed only in the real world, it could succeed. The Internet is only a different way of doing business; it hasn't rewritten the fundamentals of business. Look at the company's financials and make sure their burn rate will allow you to fulfill and contribute to the vision of the company. The Internet is a great place to be doing business right now; it will become the conduit for most business transactions in the future. The general availability in the job market of people with experience is low and opportunities are plenty for those who are familiar [with] or have experience in the industry. Though the market is volatile now, the future demands for experience will outweigh the market's ability to supply. Get in now and get experience; it will improve your marketability in the future and you might just find an exciting and fulfilling job in the process.

PETER KRENKEL, NATURAL GAS EXCHANGE
Do your market research thoroughly and analyze the data carefully. I have seen too many examples that read, "If we built this, would you use it?" A yes response by a large percentage does not necessarily provide the business case.

Above all, keep a level head. Don't fall for the wild-eyed promises that are still being made about many Internet ventures.

ANIL SABHARWAL, DESIRE2LEARN.COM
The Internet industry is not some endless goldmine. Do not count on succeeding simply because you are in the Internet industry. The fundamentals of coming up with a sound idea, ensuring that a market and need for your product or service exist, and the ability to differentiate yourself from the competition must all be carefully considered before undertaking any new initiative. It's not enough just to be in the Internet industry; you must harness its power and provide your customers with something that no one else can. And, only then, maybe you will succeed.

RICK SEGAL, MICROFORUM
The Internet, while "new" in the sense of the medium, has not changed the fundamentals. Reliability, trust, satisfaction, etc. — all the things that make that corner store successful — apply to any Internet venture. Forgetting these core values invites disaster.

Of course, it is important to pick a company with solid business fundamentals, but it is also important that the company or organization you get involved with will be progressive enough to try various things out!

MARK FOOTE, CANADIAN TIRE
I think that you want to ensure that you have the confidence in the career skills that are identified and that you work in a company that's progressive. If you have the skills, don't bang your head against the wall for too long trying to convince a company that isn't progressive to be progressive. You are too valuable somewhere else.

Think of It as a Learning Opportunity
One interesting aspect of the e-biz world is that it has encouraged many people to look at involvement in an Internet venture as merely a stepping stone in an overall career path. Rather than viewing involvement in a specific e-biz initiative as a final goal, the idea goes, you should use it as an opportunity to enhance and broaden your skills.

This theme came through clearly with a number of participants, who indicated that learning and imagination are important skills, and that the experience gained could be invaluable.

JULIE BRADSHAW, SUITE101.COM
Any new project promises the exploration and excitement of the unknown. If you look at it as an opportunity to learn and expand — as an educational experience — you will certainly come out a winner. As an added bonus, given the "newness" of the Internet, you not only have the opportunity to learn, expand, and grow, but also to contribute to its (r)evolution.

CINDY BURTON, IWAVE.COM
We are fortunate in that the Internet is allowing individuals to make fundamental changes in the way business is conducted. With our company, we have redefined the way people do research and, in course, have helped an industry evolve. We should all take this opportunity to see just how far our imaginations will allow us to go in changing business forever.

JOEL MILNE, SEASON TICKET NETWORKS
Starting an Internet company is a great experience if you're ready for the challenge. It is hard to imagine obtaining the wealth of experiences gained through any other job opportunity.

TOM WOLF, ROYAL BANK
If you're a technologist, learn the business. If you're on the business side, learn about the impact of technology and technology as a business. If you know both, you are well positioned.

Be Prepared to Make Mistakes
Many of the panellists suggested that an important career skill is the ability to take risks (more on risk in Chapter 7). And one of them mentioned, in relation to the risk issue, that you should be prepared to make mistakes.

BEN BALDWIN, CAREERXACT
Anyone entering the Internet space should be prepared to make mistakes — lots of them. What I think defines great entrepreneurs is not how many mistakes they make, but how they deal with them.

Successful entrepreneurs only make a mistake once. They learn from every one of their mistakes and the mistakes of others, and are strengthened in the process. For example, think of the most "functional" workplace in which you've been a part. Now think of the most dysfunctional. Which of these experiences would be the most powerful influence in creating your own workplace? Likely the dysfunctional one, as you made note of all that was wrong and will avoid these factors at all costs, because you've seen the negative impact. It's a stronger learning experience. This is why so many companies in Silicon Valley actually prefer to bank on people who have stuck their necks out and made mistakes.

Learn to Like Change
Getting involved with e-biz isn't just about skills and capabilities — it is also about attitude.

MARK FOOTE, CANADIAN TIRE
You gotta like change to be successful. Organizations have to be capable of embracing change — that means the leadership, the staff, the business partners, and, in many cases, the customers. E-commerce means the reduction and redefinition of jobs, relationships, and the management and flow of information.

Those things go straight at the fabric of how most companies are organized and work. You gotta like change. If you don't, you're dead.

Be Prepared for a Significant Lifestyle Change

It's also about working hard — all of these individuals have a substantial commitment to their goals.

JOEL MILNE, SEASON TICKET NETWORKS

If you are planning to change jobs to an Internet company, make sure that you are prepared for the lifestyle change that is expected. The rewards can be high and the work is challenging and enjoyable, but the demands can be high, especially on a social or family life.

VAUGHN MCINTYRE, CHARITY.CA

Before entering an Internet career, give plenty of thought to your family, social, and economic obligations. They will all take a back seat as you get consumed by the pace and demands of the Internet. Are you ready to give whatever it takes (and on many occasions it will take a lot) to make your site one of the few great success stories?

NEAL GLEDHIL, EMBRO CAPITAL NETWORK

A considerable amount of thought should go into the long-term prospects for the specific business and the specific industry, and how the Internet is affecting it and how it will change and affect it in the future. Certainly a number of companies and specific industries have a considerable amount of present risk and future risk, and a person considering entering such an environment should be suited and well prepared from a character, emotional, and financial perspective.

Have Confidence, Courage, and Conviction

Given what has happened so far with the dot-com meltdown, it can be very easy to become discouraged. Yet what drives many who get involved with e-biz is their belief in what they are doing.

ANIL SABHARWAL, DESIRE2LEARN.COM

It is essential for you (the Internet executive) to believe very strongly in your ideas, and to know that you have the ability to overcome all obstacles necessary to succeed. There will always be those who doubt your success, but you must continue to be confident — after all, if you don't believe in yourself, why would anyone else? However, the key is not to be so overconfident that you become arrogant. You must always be willing to listen to others and learn from their experiences. Every single person you meet in your lifetime knows something that you don't. Thus, if you walk away from a conversation not having learned something, you may as well have stayed in bed that day.

JASON MANN, BRAINHUNTER.COM
Most of all — have FAITH in your idea, and don't let others tell you it can't be done. The Internet is all about making new ideas work.

PETER OXLEY, REWARDSTREAM
The individual must believe so strongly in the market opportunity and their business model that it becomes almost evangelical to any people that he/she comes into contact with. In the quest for early-stage venture capital and clients, it is the norm to have ten times more negative responses than positive, so an undying conviction in your company is mandatory. However, there is a difference between fortitude of conviction and being obstinate.

Be Prepared for Uncertainty and Unpredictability

Earlier in this book, we showed that when it comes to the Internet and e-biz, change is going to be much slower than some expected. This was recognized by several members of our panel, who indicated that patience really is a virtue when it comes to the Internet.

MAURICE GATIEN, E-SPACE CONNEXIONS
If someone is coming from a mature industry, it is likely that "process" (i.e., a disciplined, established procedure) has led to a high degree of predictability. Sometimes, in the so-called old-economy company, this is very comforting, even though it can also inhibit change. Such a person should be prepared to be very flexible and to realize that a little bit of "chaos" is going to accompany them in their new career and the same predictability is not going to be present. As well, some of this unpredictability will be arriving at high speed.

GREGORY ELLIS, KANETIX.COM
Executives from more traditional or stable environments are used to a much longer decision-making cycle, and struggle with the pace of change on the Net. Therefore, before jumping into an Internet opportunity, you'd want to seriously assess your capability to handle change and whether you thrive in uncertain environments. On the upside, it's a very creative environment and the opportunities to add value to customers or processes are great.

NEAL GLEDHIL, EMBRO CAPITAL NETWORK

Initially, as the Internet was applied to various industries, business plans seemed to gel quickly. However, I believe that to be deceiving. Although the Internet world continues to develop and morph at a fast pace, patience is required to properly develop and implement a business strategy that has a sustainable competitive advantage. A considerable amount of patience is required. Although from a cursory perspective some companies, like movie stars, appear to have reached stardom overnight, there was actually a considerable amount of time and effort required to get there.

Do Your Homework!

The last pieces of advice echo our comments: Do your research.

JOHN WETMORE, IBM CANADA

I would encourage people to do their homework. Get on the Internet and check out where the hot jobs in information technology are today. In fact, if you go to IBM's site at www.can.ibm.com and click on "Job Seekers" and then on "Career Opportunities," we list all the jobs that we are currently hiring for, along with a detailed description of what job skills are required. Other leading organizations do the same. Visit those sites and understand what the job market is looking for. Clearly, demand is outstripping supply and wonderful career opportunities exist with numerous high-quality companies today. Attend career fairs, talk to recruiters and to human resources professionals for additional information.

Once you've mapped out where you want to go, you need to take a personal inventory of your own skills. Last step, identify the gaps and put a personal skills development plan in place to achieve your career goals. People should view the new, wired world as "The glass is half full, not half empty." Yes, technical skills are now a prerequisite, regardless of your profession. But let's not forget that many of the skills attributes required today have not changed. Business skills and communication skills have been important for as long as I can remember. I would suggest that we should accept change with open arms and put a personal development plan in place to make the most of it. The opportunities are there.

JOHN MACLEOD, NETTHRUPUT

It is not really a matter of someone having to change their skills and capabilities — as we commented earlier, we need people from a variety of backgrounds with a variety of skill sets to contribute to the successful operation of an e-business.

However, it is helpful for anyone wishing to participate in e-commerce to

learn what e-commerce applications, systems, and initiatives are currently
underway or planned for in their industry or specific area(s) of interest. This is
likely not too difficult to do because e-commerce is currently attracting attention
from all business sectors and from all management levels within organizations
— including the top level.

The business of e-commerce is still in its infancy, and very much a growth
sector. As a result, there are many (exciting) opportunities available to those
who wish to be involved in the changes generated by e-commerce. And, there
are still many opportunities for people to develop their expertise and become
"masters" in this field.

IDENTIFYING THE CAREER OPPORTUNITY

So where does this leave us? Well, we can't tell you where to go to find a
job. But we believe we've identified a number of issues that should give you
enough guidance to begin thinking about what you might be able to do.

The constant evolution of e-biz technologies and the Internet will
mean ongoing efforts to incorporate the best of what various new technologies will have to offer. In almost every aspect of business, we will
see the emergence of a variety of new technologies, all designed for
achieving the variety of strategic goals identified in this book. The
bottom line is that opportunity is to be had here, both in existing projects and in new projects to come.

We were inspired by a story from the *Dallas Morning News* in which
they interviewed 33-year-old Eric Hagen, who carries the title of Development Project Leader with ACS Retail Solutions. A university graduate
with a Bachelor of Arts in music education, he has carved out a career
in customer support, one of the issues we have identified as a big area
of opportunity.

When asked how he got his foot in the door, Eric replied,

In college, I starting shipping equipment for a point-of-sale company as a part-
time job. One day, they asked me to answer a customer phone call, which started
my career in customer support. Since it was a small company, I was exposed to
many different types of work, including training, software development, docu-
mentation, and installations. My work with installations got me a job at my cur-
rent company. In six years, I've worked up from installations to development
project leader.

"SUCCESS STORY," *DALLAS MORNING NEWS*, DECEMBER 17, 2000

In other words, here is a fellow who has established a unique and successful career in what is emerging as a very significant area of opportunity. We think his story is indicative of what can be done, and that people like him will have wonderful opportunities in the world of e-biz, well into the future.

Consider the nature of the opportunity before us:

- New jobs, careers, and opportunities with Internet-related companies will continue to emerge.
- Significant efforts will be made to implement new systems, with an entirely new type of specialist evolving in almost every business field.
- New positions, management and otherwise, will be created in all aspects of e-biz, particularly within large-scale organizations.
- Because the issue of e-biz is so complex, many companies will choose not to deal with it at all. Instead, they will choose to outsource e-biz efforts, leading to a new breed of external organizations.

Whatever the case may be, e-biz goes on, and opportunity will flourish.

Chapter 7

What Makes a Good Knowledge Worker?

We are in the knowledge era and it's the day of the knowledge worker.

"MELTING POT," *ECONOMIC TIMES*, SEPTEMBER 11, 2000

Part of the challenge is not getting spooked every time the press is screaming that the Internet and/or e-commerce and/or business-to-consumer is dead. Nothing has changed. Good ideas, hard work, customer acceptance, and some luck all are the same. On-line or off, the same core skills matter.

RICK SEGAL, FORMER CEO OF MICROFORUM AND CHAPTERS ONLINE

NOW THAT YOU'VE HAD A BRIEF E-BIZ REALITY CHECK AND HAVE A SENSE of where e-biz is going and where the most opportunities might be found, this is probably a good time to assess skills and attitudes that are critical to success in the wired economy. That's where this chapter comes in. In Chapter 6 we polled some of Canada's e-biz leaders and entrepreneurs about the opportunities out there. We talked to them to gain an understanding of the key career skills, attitudes, and capabilities that workers need to have today if they want to work in the e-business field.

This is important advice; our sense is that, while there is a lot of buzz about "knowledge workers" and working in the "knowledge economy," precious little guidance is available about what is really meant by those buzzwords. Pick up the newspaper, and you'll be told that we are entering the knowledge economy and you had better become a knowledge worker. Turn the page and you'll find another article, reporting that Canada is falling behind in e-biz and e-commerce, and risks missing out on the riches to be had in the dot-com economy.

WHAT THE HECK IS A KNOWLEDGE WORKER, ANYWAY?

Perhaps the most frustrating thing for people trying to figure out what they should be doing with e-biz is the lack of guidance available. They're constantly being told they had better hurry up and become knowledge workers in order to participate in the global, Internet-based economy. Yet no one seems to be able to tell them exactly what that means!

Consider some typical media coverage and headlines. First and foremost, there is no shortage of senior business leaders, politicians, and high-tech hangers-on who are all too ready to tell Canadians they had better get on board the knowledge-worker train. They remind us that it is important for our success as a nation, our personal well-being, and our overall position in the world. We're told that there is a skills shortage, but we don't know what we should be doing to take advantage of it.

We have to turn the technology and the productive capacity of the knowledge economy to our advantage.

D. H. BURNEY, PRESIDENT AND CHIEF EXECUTIVE OFFICER, CAE,
IN AN ADDRESS TO THE CANADIAN CLUB, MONTREAL, NOVEMBER 20, 2000

There really is an important role for government in making sure kids . . . have ready access to all of the Internet so they can be knowledge workers and producers in the next generation.

JOHN ADAMS, CITY OF TORONTO COUNCILLOR,
QUOTED IN A WINNIPEG NEWSPAPER

The skills of people are central to economic prosperity in the knowledge economy, so governments have to ensure that education and training, along with the opportunity for skill development and lifelong learning, are widely available. Successful economies need systems of education, training and lifelong learning.

"JOB CREATION, PRODUCTIVITY GAINS STILL KEY CHALLENGES,"
TORONTO STAR, APRIL 30, 1998

As for Canada, while it is easy to create scenarios in which emerging market economies overtake many of the industries we rely on for jobs and wealth creation today, there is no reason to fear so long as we recognize what needs to be done to be a successful knowledge economy in the global marketplace. Our worry should be whether we are doing enough to make Canada a strong knowledge economy.

"KNOWLEDGE THE KEY REQUISITE FOR DEVELOPMENT,"
TORONTO STAR, OCTOBER 11, 1998

We aren't surprised if your reaction to these admonishments is a strong desire to scream! It seems as if everyone is telling you that you've got to become a knowledge worker, but no one is bothering to tell you what a knowledge worker is, what they do, and how you can become one! To try to resolve the dilemma, we went to the popular search engine Google with the question, "What is a knowledge worker?"

The first item on the list took us to a Web page from something called the *Omnibus Dictionary*. We were advised that "a knowledge worker is a professional who performs knowledge work." Emboldened by our finding, we delved deeper into the search topic to find out what we could about "knowledge work." Maybe if we knew what that was, we could figure out what it takes to be a great knowledge worker! As we worked our way down through the search results, we were advised by one site that "Increasingly today's employers are opting to become knowledge-driven organizations; they are requiring knowledge workers."

So here is the situation as near as we can make it: To be a knowledge worker, you've got to be able to do knowledge work. And to do that type of work, you have to work for a knowledge-driven organization. It does make sense, after all, that knowledge-driven organizations need lots of knowledge workers!

What will you do day by day? Well, as we learned, you will "describe, compile, consolidate, validate, illustrate, analyze, clarify, modify, evaluate, interpret, simulate and communicate." Does that make you feel any better? Probably not — and you can blame management guru Peter Drucker for the situation we find ourselves in. It was he who coined the phrase "knowledge worker" way back in 1959.

Of course, most of us are using e-mail, the Web, and computers in our daily work. We're already knowledge workers — so why is everyone screaming at us?

LESSONS FROM THE LEADERS

To give you some good, practical guidance with respect to this issue, we once again turned to our panel from Chapter 6. We asked them, "What is the most important career skill (or attitude/personal attribute) that an executive can have in the Internet economy (or when working for a company that is being impacted by the Internet/e-commerce/e-business)?" Here's what they had to say:

Adaptability, Agility, and Flexibility

One recurring theme in the answers, which also resonates through any discussion of e-biz and the Internet, is that people must be prepared to adapt to change. That can be a challenge — many people can be significantly resistant to change, which we earlier indicated is one of the biggest barriers holding back the success of many an initiative.

But what a lot of people don't realize is that, if they are unwilling to cope with Internet-related change, their jobs, and indeed their careers, are probably going to be at risk within the next five or ten years. The digital age is demanding new abilities from people at every level, and it is demanding that they be able to deal with massive amounts of change. The bottom line is that people who can understand the changes caused around them by the wired economy, and who are willing to change with their companies, will find that this could be the key to long-term survival.

Consider the words of our experts:

JULIE BRADSHAW, SUITE101.COM
The ability to embrace the new and act on it. The ability to reach back to the old and integrate it. Experience of the past coupled with the energy and youth of the new is, in my mind, the recipe for success.

STEPHEN HUCAL, TD MARKETSITE
An individual must be flexible and re-apply his or her experience to a dynamic and unstructured environment. Due to the scope and pace of change, this industry offers extraordinary rewards, learning experience, and the opportunity to substantially impact the building of an organization from the ground up.

ARNON LEVY, GUEST-TEK
To succeed in the high-tech industry a company must be able to turn on a dime! The only advantage a small high-tech company has over larger competitors is its ability to change direction and adjust at incredible speeds. This is a tremendous advantage and the successful entrepreneur learns how to use it.

CHRIS COOK, GEARUNLIMITED.COM
An executive involved in the Internet today needs to be able to react quickly to the changing conditions of business and technology. I am not suggesting abandoning business plans or technology strategies on a whim but adapting intelligently and with thought to changes in the marketplace. . . . On the technology side, advances in CRM technology have happened so quickly that Internet

customer care will probably skip over wide-scale use of online chat and move right to Voice over IP to respond to customer inquiries. Consumers continue to log on to the Internet as millions more come on line daily. Consumers have some hesitations about purchasing and are looking for a greater sense of security about giving out credit card information. The marketplace has yet to provide the definitive solution for this problem. The Internet market is evolving daily and to be successful an executive in this industry will have to be flexible and adapt to the changes the Web is creating. The Internet by its very nature is a dynamic market and I believe in order to be a successful executive in the industry you need to be able to adapt to changes in the capital markets, technology developments, and customer demands in order to succeed.

ALBERT LAI, MYDESKTOP
The ability to change, adapt, and be nimble. The ability to have the courage to value speed over comfort. The ability to inhibit one's perfectionism to unleash one's sheer desire for speed. To win as a start-up, as "David," your only weapon is speed, flexibility, and creativity. This means you must be ready and willing to change on a dime and be open to try things that have never been done before.

ALBERT WAHBE, E-SCOTIA
As the e-commerce revolution unfolds, it is important for individuals to embrace change with enthusiasm. With the rapid pace of the changes taking place on the Web, employees need to be able to adapt quickly. It is critical for these individuals to translate the changes taking place into benefits for their business by using technology to provide business solutions.

SHAWNEE LOVE, STOCKHOUSE MEDIA
It's a tie between the ability to see the big picture and the ability to adapt. It is a circle really. Adaptability enables an individual to see the big picture, which enables a person to adapt, and so on. I view seeing the big picture as vital, because it enables people to use their judgment to make decisions that objectively consider many different factors and it promotes creativity. Adaptability ensures the person can learn, grow, develop, and take risks, all of which are important in a new media economy. An adage for our world in general is "grow or die." Lack of these two qualities result in missing the opportunities (either from not seeing them or not acting once you've seen them), which means no growth. No growth is stagnation. Stagnation is death — or might as well be to people in this economy.

EMAD RIZKALLA, ZEDDCOMM

Nothing is set in stone in this industry and things move very fast — inflexible or stubborn executives will not be able to morph and adapt to survive. Dealing effectively with uncertainty is a prerequisite for the industry.

CINDY BURTON, iWAVE.COM

The ability to change quickly is clearly the most important skill for any executive in the Internet industry. Too often people rely on what has worked in the past or what is familiar and that, while it might keep you from failing, will not likely take you to the head of the pack.

SUHAYYA ABU-HAKIMA, AMIKANOW!

The most important skill that I have demonstrated in the Internet economy is that of entrepreneurial flexibility. My wireless Internet company, AmikaNow!, is delivering very different technology than what I expected when I wrote my first business plan two years ago. Our vision is still that of simplifying technology for people, but what we are delivering is technology such as AmikaFreedom.com, which allows people to stay in touch with their key information anywhere, anytime, and in any place. Instead of only unifying their information in a portal, we are intelligently interpreting it and moving what is important to them while they are mobile.

SYED HASAN, RESPONSETEK NETWORKS

Predictive flexibility. What I mean by this is the ability to constantly be re-evaluating one's business model and strategy in the context of the rapidly changing Internet environment and continually reinvent products and services that enable one's core service offering to remain relevant. If an executive can develop a culture of predictive flexibility within the organization, then these rapid small shifts will be embraced by the organization rather than rejected as "uncertainty of vision."

JOHN WETMORE, IBM CANADA

As we all know, technology is ubiquitous and touches every walk of life today. To me, one of the most essential attributes/skills required to succeed in the wired world today is to be open-minded and flexible to new approaches and in the use of Internet technology to help you achieve your objectives — whether you are an artist, a doctor, a business leader, or a volunteer. Business skills and an understanding of how business works are also important, as are communications and being able to effectively express your ideas with customers or peers.

Communications ties it all together. Other attributes that come to mind are creativity and innovative thinking, being a team player, and an enthusiastic, positive attitude when faced with change or new challenges. The model employee also demonstrates passion for the business.

JONATHAN EHRLICH, MOBSHOP
The key ingredient to any successful Internet opportunity is being comfortable with the pace of change. . . . In the Internet space, business models can change within a 24-hour period and your business can go from being incredibly successful to being an absolute dog. You need to be incredibly flexible, you need to be incredibly even-keeled, and you need to be able to move at the pace of the change. That, for people coming out of traditional industries, is the largest single barrier to their success. . . . You have to be able to deal with massive, massive amounts of uncertainty and enormous shades of grey. . . . If you can't feel comfortable walking out of a meeting more confused than walking in, then you shouldn't be in this new economy, certainly in early-stage companies . . . maybe with larger companies it's probably a little less dramatic. But in early-stage organizations, you have to be able to deal with shades of grey the size of the Grand Canyon.

ANDREA REISMAN, FORMER CEO, PETOPIA.COM
The single most important skill set is intellectual and organizational dexterity. The ability to comprehend and respond to change is critical in this rapidly morphing environment.

JOSEPH CARUSONE, STOCKHOUSE MEDIA
Anyone that wants to work for an Internet company absolutely needs to be able to cope with a rapidly changing environment. This includes the physical environment (our Toronto office is moving this week for the third time in 14 months), the competitive environment (new competitors emerge and disappear on an almost daily basis), and the internal business environment (we need to be able to pursue new opportunities and cut out nonperforming endeavours very rapidly). I tell all prospective employees that, if they like to know exactly what their days will be like, then StockHouse is not the place for them. There are no comfortable pigeonholes here!

An Open Mind

An aspect of adaptability and flexibility is the ability to keep an open mind. Far too many people are, when presented with something new, too willing to discount it or dismiss it. That's the type of attitude that can get you in trouble in the e-biz age.

MARVIN IGELMAN, BRANDERA.COM
I feel that an Internet exec should above all keep an open mind. The Internet has created all types of opportunities and business models that were non-existent only a short time ago. The ability to listen to a new idea or accept a new concept is vital to the success of a new-economy company. Internet execs should be able to quickly navigate their companies through the ever-changing landscape that they will face. This requires the ability to turn on a dime in many circumstances. This can only be achieved if the exec is open-minded enough to, in many cases, try the unconventional.

ALBERT WAHBE, E-SCOTIA
[People] need to be open-minded to the unlimited opportunities created by the Internet and the advantages of e-commerce for their company. Selling on the Web can make a significant difference to their bottom line and open the doors to new markets on a global scale. It is also critical for these individuals to be able to think differently about how they do business and how they can benefit from the convenience of selling to new markets using the Web. They will need to develop a strategy on how they can "Webitize" their business — transform services and processes to offer their customers more choice in how they want to do business.

Creativity and Vision
E-biz is also about thinking differently. The phrase "thinking out of the box" has long been part of business jargon, but nowhere is the need for originality and creativity when approaching a business issue more important than with the Internet. Part of creative thinking about the Internet is trying to figure out the new business models and ways of doing business that it might make possible. This can be difficult, in that the concept of business models for the Internet is often obscured by buzzwords. Consider this quote, for example:

Our mission is to provide customized, flexible, high-quality, innovative products that will allow efficient and effective dissemination of newly-discovered market-driven paradigms allowing pro-active management that underpins corporate success.

"BUZZWORD BABBLE RULES," *NEW STRAITS TIMES*, APRIL 4, 2001

Uh-huh. If you can understand the phrase above, you've mastered new-economy speak. If you can't — join the rest of us. You are probably as frustrated as we are by the silly rhetoric that so often surrounds ventures related to the Internet.

There has been much talk about changing business models over the past few years, but we think that it has only obscured the opportunities to be found online. From our perspective, the new business models are not defined by the buzzwords that have infested the Internet and e-commerce over the past few years. Indeed, the buzzwords often hide what is really going on. Such jargon has clouded the view of online opportunity to such an extent that many people involved in e-biz are still wondering what exactly the phrase "Internet business models" means. They are confused and misdirected about where the real potential of the Internet lies.

Worse yet, they have stopped using their creativity, since they have come to think that the Internet and e-biz involve only a cookie-cutter approach to business. In other words, buzzwords kill vision. E-biz is so complex that every situation is different. Can we expect to define a business model and easily apply it to any one company? Could we come up with a model such as an e-marketplace and presume that it should apply to every industry and every company? Does B2C make sense for everyone? No, no, and no.

The problem with cookie-cutter solutions and with the e-biz hype of the day is that they obscure the vast complexity of what is underway in the business world. The buzzwords that swarm out of the high-tech and e-biz industries like bees out of a hive conceal much of the change that is going on — the change is so complex and so vast. In the business world there are often huge disparities between companies and between industries. What is important to one organization might not be to another. How can we possibly expect a simple premise compressed into a buzzword to apply to a world that is so complicated?

All too often the use of buzzwords indicates a simplistic approach to new ways of conducting business that are possible with the Internet. Given the vast differences found in many industries, these cookie-cutter approaches don't and won't work. What is required instead is creativity in the way that people envision the opportunities of e-biz. Consider what our panellists had to say on this issue:

MARK FOOTE, CANADIAN TIRE

You have to be creative. E-commerce is not about the reinstitutionalization of your existing business model using a new vehicle. The power in e-commerce is thinking about how the new opportunity can be used to rethink your business assumptions. Where is value created? Who makes money and why? How can the brand be levered or extended? What new intermediation or disintermediation schemes can be created? How can your assets be levered in new ways (e.g., your buildings, brand, intellectual capital, etc.)? And most importantly, how can you use e-commerce to entrench stronger business-partner and customer relationships?

NEAL GLEDHIL, EMBRO CAPITAL NETWORK

For the most part, developing and running a business with the Internet as an integral part of your business plan involves operating "outside of the box." You need to be able to speculate, with the best information you have on hand at that time, where things are headed and/or where you can take things as far as your specific business and your industry. You never have all the information you may prefer or tended to have when you used to make corporate strategy decisions, and the Internet changes on an uncommonly fast and continual spectrum. As a result, it is continual creativity that is required to carve out a competitive advantage and maintain it.

TOM WOLF, ROYAL BANK

In terms of management, they have to be visionary, politically savvy, and understand the key drivers or levers of the business.

SCOTT RANKINE, METAMAIL

The ability to look beyond moment-to-moment events, to see new opportunities where others see only problems or nothing at all.

CHRIS KLOTZ, JOBSHARK.COM

A broad vision, with the ability to apply sound traditional business practices, while utilizing all the economies that the Internet provides to improve economies of scale, competitive advantage, and profitability.

Leadership Skills

Leadership in the Internet era requires unique skills: the ability to envision a future unlike anything of the past; the skill to motivate employees to cope with a dramatic period of change; and the intelligence and wisdom to establish strategies in a world of business that seems no longer to make sense. One of our panellists, sensing that the best way to cope with change is to inspire change, indicated that he believed this leadership issue to be the most important. He called it "adaptive strategic leadership."

STEPHEN HUCAL, TD MARKETSITE
In an industry with few existing models, an executive in the Internet industry must provide adaptive strategic leadership for the company. What does adaptive strategic leadership mean? An executive must, in real-time mode, utilize the experience, business skills, and knowledge residing within the organization to define and continually adjust the objective and competitive strategy for the company. Unlike other industries, the Internet is constantly evolving, based on new technology and market changes. An executive must be a catalyst for change within the organization and nurture a culture that continually learns and adapts to changes in its environment. The principles of business remain the same, but the formulas for success evolve with the technology and people.

SCOTT RANKINE, METAMAIL
Even the best battle plan needs someone to rally the troops and lead the charge. The best kinds of leaders inspire their people to action, the worst intimidate them.

There are many facets to leadership. One of the most important is good communication skills. When dealing with something that is new, cutting-edge, and innovative, it can often take a lot of hard work to "inspire the troops" or get potential investors on side. Hence, many of our panellists looked at leadership from the communication perspective.

JOEL MILNE, SEASON TICKET NETWORKS
As a founder of an Internet company you will need to "sell" your company to everyone — investors, partners, employees, contractors, etc. If you can't effectively communicate why your company is going to be wildly successful, and people don't believe in you, then it will be virtually impossible to get off the ground, no matter how good your product or idea is (unless you've developed a terabit wireless handheld device — then don't worry about it!). Convincing people why your idea is going to work is crucial and it is a process that you will have to continually improve, based on feedback, analysis, and personal experience.

JASON MANN, BRAINHUNTER.COM

It doesn't matter what role you are playing as an executive, you'll need to effectively communicate the company's ideas, products, goals, position, etc., and sell people on the concept. Whether it's written or in person or in speaking engagements or in interviews, you need to sell. Most Internet companies are new, so their concepts tend to be unproven. You need to create excitement among your customers and your staff to enable them to sell your concepts.

BRUCE LINTON, WEBHANCER

In this business (even more than the previous life of telecommunication network management software), selling a concept well has been the biggest benefit. I view this requirement as leading and defining of the successful CEO, as everything we are doing is without direct comparison for value and application. In selling how webHancer will improve the way the World Wide Web delivers, it is critical, as in all business, to know what you have to deliver and when the balance will arrive, but concept selling has been the number-one skill to date.

A Grab Bag of Other Requirements

Some panellists identified a range of other important issues, each of which speaks for itself:

- **Management experience**

R. J. (BOB) HUGGINS, COLD NORTH WIND

The first and foremost attribute is the knowledge of who Topo Gigio was. And if a promising exec answers, "It was the mouse that bid 'Kiss me goodnight, Eddie' on the Ed Sullivan Show," it is of course a measure of a maturity level needed to succeed and exceed in an Internet environment. Whether it is an Internet-based or traditional bricks-and-mortar business, the same business basics are required. Form a strong team of individuals with complementary skill sets. Lean on your local business network for individuals who have "been there, done that." Our greatest accomplishment in that area was attracting Bob Allum, a co-founder of Jetform Inc., as our chairman. When hiring personnel, I like well-rounded, well-travelled, university-educated individuals. Generalists are important to round out your technical personnel.

- **Diversity and well-roundedness**

JOHN MACLEOD, NETTHRUPUT

In our organization, employees represent a broad range of backgrounds and skill sets. This diversity contributes to the successful operation of our e-business.

We have found that to operate an e-business successfully requires not only knowledge and expertise in the "e" side of the business, but also in all of the other disciplines that are applied to effectively run most any other enterprise. If there is a common thread that runs through the organization, it is that we are all ready to learn new things, adapt to change, and apply all the tools and resources we have on hand to move us forward.

MALA GUNADASA, ESEEDS.COM
I think it is important that an individual be an all-round type of person, someone who is skilled in many different areas. He doesn't have to be an expert in all of them, of course, but should at least know the basics in many different areas so that he can coordinate the work and call in experts where necessary. This also ensures flexibility of skills and a willingness and ability to learn new things quickly, as they are presented (they always are!).

• Marketing, technology, and negotiation skills
MARK FOOTE, CANADIAN TIRE
I think that the three most important career skills are to be fluent in marketing, technology, and the ability to influence and negotiate. Marketing and technology are critical because, along with the attributes listed above, they combine to create vision. Technologists who can't market and marketing folk who don't understand technology aren't in a position to lead or drive the changes in companies. Influencing skills are critical, simply because e-commerce requires you to influence change in people's thinking, in company economics, etc.

COLIN WEBSTER, EDEAL COMMERCE NETWORK
The Internet economy has no hierarchy. Because deals need to be done fast, you have to enter negotiations with a win-win-for-everyone attitude, where both parties look out for both parties. Everybody is your friend because change is difficult, and one day you're up and the next you are down.

• Curiosity
MAURICE GATIEN, E-SPACE CONNEXIONS
The most important quality is curiosity. Curiosity breeds flexibility and ensures that an enlightened executive does not weld himself or herself to a particular method or to a particular "appliance." Curiosity also keeps the executive modest, since the realization rapidly sets in that one only knows a fraction of what is needed. Parallel with this quality, it is important to project this curiosity to employees and colleagues, since they can share their sometimes different perspectives in

an atmosphere where new information and opinions are welcomed, not stifled. Curiosity keeps things fresh — and more fun.

• Ability to attract talented employees

DAVID F. MASOTTI, SKULOGIX

The most important skill an executive working in the Internet industry must have is the ability to attract outstanding talent across all functional areas. Good ideas are a dime a dozen and not that hard to come up with. What is difficult to come up with is a group of people that can put flesh on the bones and execute a plan. I prefer to build an organization from the top down, bringing in senior, experienced talent, and then fill in the organization underneath them. It is important to choose the smartest people you can find, but also people that fit together culturally. Any good venture capitalist will tell you that good ideas backed by an outstanding management team will always get financed, no matter what the market conditions. While you are pre-revenue, the only real asset you have is human assets — settling for anything less than the most talented people you can find anywhere is a mistake.

• Ability to sift through significant quantities of information

With the emergence of the Internet, we have virtually begun to drown in information. Learning how to research and synthesize this vast quantity of data was identified by some as being the most important and useful career skill.

VAUGHN MCINTYRE, CHARITY.CA

In my opinion, the most important skill an Internet executive can have is the ability to adjust to significant quantities of information, stimuli, and competitive threats. If an executive can adapt, filter, stay focused, and change, based on a constantly changing business landscape, then they at least have a chance to participate in the success of an Internet company.

JOE DALES, FARMS.COM

In my experience, it is the ability to interpret a huge amount of information and distill it down to an action plan that accomplishes the strategic vision and objectives.

• Risk-taking attitude

Another common theme was that people must be willing to take risks.

MARK FOOTE, CANADIAN TIRE

[People] need to have a bit of a "Wild West" orientation. The structures and models that are emerging are the result of folks who pioneer new thinking and investment. For big companies, being fast followers into the Wild West can work well.

You have to be brave. Given that the leverage in e-commerce is most powerful in the redefinition of how a company works, it's a natural boat-rocker for the status quo. Companies who don't have the stones to charge ahead are doomed.

PETER OXLEY, REWARDSTREAM

Many start-ups get overtaken by swift-footed competitors that are able to be proactive to the changing needs of the Internet consumer. The Internet never sleeps and is constantly morphing the way we do business. It will be mandatory to make tweaks and changes to your business model — your business plan should be a living, breathing document. Many companies get obsessed with staunchly defending their current mode of doing business, and get blindsided by a quantum leap in Internet technology or a new competitor. Stand by your convictions, but marry this with an ability to constantly innovate within your business.

TOM WOLF, ROYAL BANK

In terms of implementing e-biz projects I would look for people that "get things done" and are a bit of risk-takers.

To suggest that a bit of risk-taking is required in the e-biz economy might seem a bit far-fetched. After all, we've just been through a time in which a tremendous number of people took massive risks — and failed spectacularly. And yet, in dealing with the potential for change that the Internet and e-biz represent, it is clear that risk-taking is required.

That is perhaps one of the most dangerous aspects of the dot-com collapse — people's attitudes towards risk-taking are changing. After the way the dot-com death march overwhelmed the business world, we run the risk that too many people will lose their willingness to take chances and innovate. Venture capitalists, burned by the collapse of their investments, have tuned out of the technology industry and might not be back for some time. In the corporate sector, e-commerce visionaries are hiding in the back rooms, afraid to suggest to their bosses that some type of online strategy be pursued. Business leaders are too shell-shocked by their collapsing share prices to dare even mention the Internet in their annual report.

No one wants to take a risk because the climate is ugly, which is a terrible thing, given the long-term impact of the Internet. The fact is, innovation is a good thing. With the Internet and e-biz, we believe that a new form of corporate R&D will soon be mandatory, across the board, for all organizations. Companies are going to have to invest heavily in continuous exploration of new ways of doing business via the Internet, even though they may be uncertain as to their eventual return, because competitive necessity will force them to.

The reason for this is that there is a conundrum at work with the Internet. While much broad guidance about online business strategies makes sense, it is difficult to pinpoint with any accuracy the specific business model or strategy that will work for a particular company, industry, or situation. To best apply the Internet to any individual situation requires tinkering and experimenting with the new business models it provides. The only way to figure out which ones make absolute sense is to try them out — and that requires taking a risk.

From that perspective, we believe that the idea of business-model R&D will gain credence and become a required component of corporate spending. Companies in the ever-changing business world are going to have to experiment continuously with new ways of doing business that are based upon the technology of the Internet. They will go into this research fully understanding that the various things they try might not work, and that much of it could fail. Companies have always had to invest in R&D to invent new products and services, with the understanding that some research will produce winners and much will produce losers. So too will they have to invest R&D money into new business models and e-biz initiatives, which is why a risk-taking attitude is still very important — a good thought as we lead into the close of this book.

Chapter 8

Never Look Back

It's going to be very much harder than you thought.

HERMAN TURKSTRA, 701.COM

T HIS IS THE MOST DIFFICULT BOOK WE HAVE EVER TRIED TO WRITE, AND that's no understatement. We began this project early in the spring of 2000, aiming to provide an overview of the business realities and opportunities of the Internet and e-commerce. We were skeptical about much of what we saw occurring, and thought it important to write a book that returned to the real business fundamentals of the Internet. Much of that material ended up as the basis for chapters 6 and 7.

At the time, the dot-com and investment-market hysteria was in full swing. We found ourselves frequently banging our heads against the wall and yelling that things were going too far.

Then began the collapse. We secretly felt pleased about the ensuing market crash in April 2000 and the following dot-com meltdown. This, we reasoned, would make reality set in, and people would get back to the fundamentals of e-biz. But, as we noted earlier, things swung too far the other way. The negativity that began to swirl around anything technology-related became a big — no, a huge challenge for us as we worked on this book.

With so much doom and gloom surrounding us, how could we motivate ourselves to write about e-biz and the Internet? How could we talk about re-engineering business transactions, when so many high-tech companies were struggling? How could we write about the emerging opportunity of customer service and support, when dot-com pioneers in this area were disappearing? It was difficult, but slowly the tone of the book began to change. It evolved from a discussion of business strategy to one on business strategy mixed with a strong reality check.

And one thing kept us going — our passion for and belief in the Internet.

We've been at this a long time. Jim Carroll has been online since 1982, and Rick Broadhead since the early nineties. Together we've penned 30 books. We look back on each with pride, and the feedback on them tells us we have done a good job in helping people understand the nature of e-biz and the Internet.

Our intent has always been to help people understand how they can take advantage of particular Internet and e-biz technologies and opportunities. However, like many whose careers depend on information technology, e-biz, and the Internet, we've gone through 2001 feeling rather battered and bruised by the shift in popular opinion caused by the dot-com collapse. Looking back as we close off this project, we've realized that, in order to move forward with the real potential of e-biz and the Internet, you must have a rather thick skin.

And you must have passion. Given that many online business strategies still make sense, it should come as no surprise that, despite the dot-com meltdown, countless numbers of people still continue to believe passionately in the potential of the online world. You are probably among them, as are we. If you are not, you should be. People are testing their passion for e-biz and the Internet on a daily basis, by constantly assessing and exploring what can be done with it.

That, perhaps more than anything, is a key reason why the Internet will continue to change business models dramatically over the long run and to affect the economy and the way that business is conducted. A huge amount of drive, imagination, talent, and effort continues to be devoted to the Internet, particularly within existing companies. People are still exploring opportunities and actively seeking to apply technology to business problems or to use technology to achieve a competitive advantage.

It was a curious juxtaposition, but we found that the amount of attention given to e-commerce within the corporate sector had increased by the time the dot-com meltdown was underway. People are examining the way that business is conducted in almost every industry — or within their own companies — and are setting out to apply e-business technologies within those industries and companies in order to take advantage of the widespread connectivity that exists online. Sure, they can't be certain that the business models they are exploring will be successful, and there is no doubt that many new, Internet-based business models have failed. But, regardless of the fact that success is uncertain, countless new models are undeniably being explored, tested, and tried out — and the bottom line is that some will "stick."

All because people have passionate belief. What drives them? Their belief that they are doing the right thing. Let's go back to the panellists from the previous chapters. One of them, Ben Baldwin of careerXact, stated it best:

The best Internet executives have more than just hard "skills." They have something far more important that drives them to success — and it's not something they learned at Harvard or Stanford. It's passion. Passion tied with absolute conviction and focus in their vision.

Passion and focus help any entrepreneur become successful, but in the Internet industry this is absolutely essential. Why? Because chances are, if you've created something truly revolutionary, you're going to face some strong opposition, as change is not always welcomed with open arms.

You're going somewhere no one else has gone before. It's your job to guide your partners, employees, and investors. They will expect you to know the way before you've ever been down the path. Use your passion, belief, and conviction to guide you. The ones who pretend to hold a map are likely more lost than you.

The good news is, the harder it gets, the more chance there is for greater success, as fewer people will walk that path.

There is one other important lesson to learn. As you are assessing your opportunities, don't dwell on the Internet period of 1994 to 2000. Instead, take the long view, cast your mind forward, and think about the real opportunity that is yet to come. As one of our panellists, Anil Sabharwal of Desire2Learn.com, stated,

Never look back — the road is forward. If you spend too much time reflecting on what's been done, you're not spending enough time on what could be done.

And what about the Internet and e-biz? The best is yet to come. We passionately believe that to be true, and so should you.

Appendix:
Our Panel of Leaders

THESE ARE THE PEOPLE WHOSE OPINIONS WE SOLICITED FOR CHAPTERS 6 AND 7.

SUHAYYA (SUE) ABU-HAKIMA
Founder and CEO, AmikaNow!
Industry: e-mail management software solutions and services
Web Site: www.amikanow.com

BEN BALDWIN
Chief Executive Officer, careerXact
Industry: online job candidate screening service
Web Site: www.careerxact.com

JULIE BRADSHAW
Co-founder and Managing Director, Suite101.com
Industry: Web directory services
Web Site: www.suite101.com

CINDY BURTON
President, iWave.com
Industry: information research services
Web Site: www.iwave.com

JOSEPH CARUSONE
Senior Vice-President, StockHouse Media
Industry: financial services
Web Site: www.stockhouse.com

CHRIS COOK
President and CEO, gearunlimited.com
Industry: online portal and retailer for action/adventure sports
Web Site: www.gearunlimited.com

JOE DALES
Founder and Senior Vice-President, Marketing, Farms.com
Industry: e-business solutions provider for the agriculture industry
Web Site: www.farms.com

JONATHAN EHRLICH
Co-founder and Vice-President, MobShop
Industry: provider of demand aggregation technology for public and private marketplaces
Web Site: www.mobshop.com

GREGORY ELLIS
Co-founder, kanetix.com
Industry: insurance
Web Site: www.kanetix.com

MARK FOOTE
President, Canadian Tire Retail
Industry: retailer (home products, automotive, sports and leisure)
Web Site: www.canadiantire.ca

MAURICE GATIEN
Chief Executive Officer, e-SPACE CONNEXIONS
Industry: online solutions provider for the Canadian commercial real estate market
Web Site: www.e-space.com

NEAL GLEDHIL
Chairman, CEO, and Director, EMBRO Capital Network
Industry: online investment banking
Web Site: www.embro.com

MALA GUNADASA
President and Founder, eSeeds.com
Industry: online retailer of seeds
Web Site: www.eseeds.com

SYED HASAN
President and CEO, Responsetek Networks
Industry: customer experience management software
Web Site: www.responsetek.com

OMID HODAIE
President and CEO, Isopia
Industry: e-learning infrastructure software
Web Site: www.isopia.com

STEPHEN HUCAL
President and CEO, TD MarketSite
Industry: online trading portal for Canadian businesses
Web Site: www.tdmarketsite.com

R. J. (BOB) HUGGINS
President and CEO, Cold North Wind
Industry: digitization services for microfilm collections
Web Site: www.coldnorthwind.com

MARVIN IGELMAN
President and CEO, BrandEra.com
Industry: business-to-business portal for creative marketing and
advertising professionals
Web Site: www.brandera.com

CHRISTOPHER KLOTZ
Chief Executive Officer, Jobshark.com
Industry: online recruitment services
Web Site: www.jobshark.com

PETER KRENKEL
President, Natural Gas Exchange
Industry: electronic trading and clearing services for the natural gas
industry
Web Site: www.ngx.com

ALBERT LAI
Co-founder, MyDesktop
Industry: computing portal
Web Site: www.mydesktop.com

ARNON LEVY
President and CEO, Guest-Tek
Industry: broadband Internet solutions for the hospitality industry
Web Site: www.guesttek.com

BRUCE LINTON
President, webHancer
Industry: Web site performance software
Web Site: www.webhancer.com

SHAWNEE LOVE
Human Resources Manager, StockHouse Media
Industry: financial services
Web Site: www.stockhouse.com

JOHN MACLEOD
President and CEO, NetThruPut (formerly Enbridge Petroleum Exchange)
Industry: Internet-based crude-oil trading systems
Web Site: www.netthroughput.com

JASON MANN
Co-founder and EVP, Product and Operations, Brainhunter.com
Industry: Web-based recruiting
Web Site: www.brainhunter.com

DAVID MASOTTI
Director, Skulogix
Industry: online channel-management solutions
Web Site: www.skulogix.com

VAUGHN MCINTYRE
Partner and CEO, Charity.ca
Industry: online charity portal
Web Site: www.charity.ca

PAUL MERCIA
President and CEO, Cybersurf
Industry: Internet service provider/software development
Web Site: www.cybersurf.ca

JOEL MILNE
President and CTO, Season Ticket Networks
Industry: online season-ticket software
Web Site: www.tickethippo.com, www.seasonticketnetworks.com

PETER OXLEY
President and Co-founder, RewardStream
Industry: online loyalty solutions provider
Web Site: www.rewardstream.com

SCOTT RANKINE
President and CEO, Metamail
Industry: electronic mail and graphics compression software
Web Site: www.metamail.com

ANDREA REISMAN
Founder and former CEO, Petopia.com
[Petopia.com was acquired by Petco Animal Supplies in December 2000.]
Industry: online pet supplies retailer
Web Site: www.petopia.com, www.petco.com

EMAD RIZKALLA
President, ZeddComm
Industry: information technology solutions
Web Site: www.zeddcomm.com

ANIL SABHARWAL
Co-founder, Desire2Learn.com
Industry: online educational solutions
Web Site: www.desire2learn.com

RICK SEGAL
President and CEO, Microforum
Industry: e-business solutions provider
Web Site: www.microforum.com

DUSHYANT SHARMA
Chairman and Chief Technology Officer, Derivion
Industry: online billing
Web Site: www.derivion.com

BOB TAPSCOTT
Senior Vice-President, Strategy, Maptuit
Industry: wireline and wireless Internet location-based services
Web Site: www.maptuit.com

HERMAN TURKSTRA
Chief Executive Officer, 701.com
Industry: community Web site provider; independent business
telephone directory publisher
Web Site: www.701.com

ALBERT WAHBE
Chairman and CEO, e-Scotia
Industry: financial services
Web Site: www.e-scotia.com

COLIN WEBSTER
President, edeal Commerce Network
Industry: online marketplace service provider
Web Site: www.edeal.com

JOHN WETMORE
President and CEO, IBM Canada
Industry: information technology solutions
Web Site: www.ibm.com/canada

TOM WOLF
Senior Vice-President of eBusiness, Royal Bank
Industry: financial services
Web Site: www.royalbank.com

Index

Abu-Hakima, Suhayya, 172, 188
accounting, 79, 117
AccPac, 117–18
ACS Retail Solutions, 180
Adams, John, 184
advertising industry, 99
Air Canada, 125, 145, 147
aircanadasucks.com, 129
airline industry, 133–34, 136.
   See also specific airlines
Allum, Bob, 194
Amazon.com, 12, 59, 142
American Association of
   Advertising Agencies, 99
AmikaNow!, 188. *See also*
   Abu-Hakima, Suhayya
Analog Devices, 119–20
Andreessen, Marc, 47, 61
Answers.com, 148
Apollo space program, 80–81
application service providers,
   78
Ariba Buyer, 37–38
Arthur Andersen, 79
auctions, online, 74
auto industry, 18, 53
  impact of Internet on, 72
  inventory management in,
   95, 119

Baldwin, Ben, 176, 201
banking, online, 18, 19, 126
Bayer Silicones. *See* GE Plastics

Beckman, Wayne, 40
Ben and Jerry's, 145–47
Bezos, Jeff, 12
BigBook, 31
Blackberry pager, 59
Blue Martini, 41–42
boats.com, 14–15
Bradshaw, Julie, 172, 175, 186
Brainhunter.com. *See* Mann, Jason
BrandEra.com. *See* Igelman,
   Marvin
Brightspark, 32
Bristol-Myers Squibb, 122
Broadhead, Rick, viii–ix, 200,
   218–19
Broadvision, 156
budgeting, 95
BuildStores, 34
Burney, D. H., 184
Burton, Cindy, 176, 188
business models
  of dot-coms, 78–79, 200–201
  first-to-market, 61–63
  need for old-economy rules in,
   65–66
  new, 74, 97, 188, 190–92
  R&D for, 198
  re-evaluating, 188, 197
business plans, 173–74
business processes
  checks and balances in, 56–57
  and e-commerce
   implementation, 38, 95

outsourcing of, 77–79
re-engineering of, 119–20, 167
and U.S. space program, 80–81
business service providers, 78–79
business theory, 80–81
B2B applications, 12–13, 36–37
costs of, 43
customer support in, 154–55
failure of, 53
hype around, 74
integration of, 38, 43
potential benefits of, 93–94
software for, 36–38
B2C applications, 38. *See also*
shopping, online
business-to-business e-commerce.
See B2B applications
business-to-consumer e-commerce.
See B2C applications
Business Week, 30
buyer-driven pricing, 74
buzzwords, 190–91

Cahners In-Stat Group, 127
Calgary Herald, 142
call centres, 125, 130–31, 132.
See also customer service
and online customer support,
134, 136
Canada Post, 100–101
Canadian Binnacle, 15
Canadian Facts, 19
Canadian Internet Handbook
(Carroll and Broadhead), 5
Canadian Tire, 41–43. *See also*
Foote, Mark
CAP Ventures, 90
careers, e-business
as learning opportunities,
175–76
need for commitment in, 177
opportunities for, 165–66,
168–69, 179–81
security in, 165–66
careerXact. *See* Baldwin, Ben

Carroll, Jim, vii–viii, 66, 200, 220–21
Carusone, Joseph, 189
cellphones. *See* m-commerce
Ceridian Canada, 78
CF Group, 19
change
attitude towards, 176–79,
186–89, 197
and corporate culture, 50–54,
120–21, 167–68, 176–77
costs of, 98
and the Internet, 20–21
lifestyle, 177
organizational, 79, 88, 120–21
pace of, 56–57, 63, 81–82,
178–79, 186
Chapters, 142
Chapters.ca, 38–39
Charity.ca. *See* McIntyre, Vaughn
Charles Schwab, 19, 52
CheckFree, 101
checks and balances, 56–57
Chevron, 99
Chong, Lim, 35
CIBC, 78
Clarify, 143
Colbeth, Doug, 31
Cold North Wind. *See* Huggins,
R. J. (Bob)
communication, 80–81
as business skill, 188–89, 193–94
effects of technology on, 81–82
comparison shopping, 138
competition, 126–29, 137–38
computers
and Internet access, 57–59
and the paperless office, 88–91
consultants, 166, 167. *See also*
outsourcing
consumers
empowerment of, 72–73,
128–29, 138–39, 161
resistance to change of, 47–48
convergence, 60–61
Cook, Chris, 174, 186

Cooper, Jack, 122
Coopers & Lybrand, 89
corporate culture. *See also*
  corporate knowledge
  and change, 50–54, 120–21,
    167–68, 176–77
  and customer service, 161
  need for coordination in,
    135–36, 156
  need for education in, 118
  and values, 170–71
corporate knowledge, 132, 157–60
Covisint, 53
credit cards, 60, 187. *See also*
  security
CRM. *See* customer relationship
  management
currency, virtual, 60
customer-contact systems. *See also*
  call centres
  need for integration in, 136–37,
    140, 160–61
  problems with, 136
  staff needs for, 133–35
customer relationship
  management (CRM), 137, 140,
    160–61, 186–87. *See also*
  customer service
customers. *See also* consumers
  expectations of, 94, 121, 124–29,
    137, 158
  information centres for, 139,
    143–60
  loyalty of, 131
  relationships with, 93–94, 129,
    192
  self-service by, 108–16, 130, 139,
    147
customer service, 73–74, 138–61,
    186–87. *See also* call centres
  benefits of, 130–32
  dissatisfaction with, 124,
    132–33
  by e-mail, 124–25, 130–31, 133,
    136, 139–43

failure of, 132–37
  by Voice over IP, 186–87
Cybercash, 60
Cyber Dialogue, 24

Daily Telegraph, 23
Dales, Joe, 196
Dean Foods, 107
Dell Computers, 37–38, 73, 126–27
Delphi Communications, 159
Dennis, Gary, 49
Derivion, 101
Desire2Learn.com. *See* Sabharwal,
  Anil
Digicash, 60
Digital Systems Report, 79
Discover, 81
disintermediation, 15, 17, 192
Documentum, 156
Dorchak, Glenda M., 65
dot-com collapse, 5, 13–14, 22, 173
  benefits of, 82–83
  causes of, 46, 53, 66–67
  impact of, 197, 199–200
  perspective on, 26–27, 63
DotComFailures, 13
dotcomgraveyard.com, 13
dot-coms. *See also* dot-com
  collapse
  millionaires created by, 21–22
  weaknesses of, 133
Dow Jones Interactive, 30, 222
Drucker, Peter, 165, 185

e-billing, 46, 75–76, 92
  benefits of, 102
  clearinghouses for, 100–101
  by Microsoft, 98–99
  software for, 101
  systems for, 100–103
EBPP. *See* e-billing
e-business. *See also* B2B and B2C
  applications; careers,
  e-business; e-commerce
  advantages of, 93–96

and change, 176–77, 186–89,
195
complexity of, 33–40, 63
and confidence, 175, 177–78
cost savings of, 46, 49, 74–76,
93, 116, 121
costs of implementing, 40–44
and flexibility, 167–68, 178–79,
189–90, 195, 196
implementation of, 37–38
need for, 63–65
and passion, 171–72, 189,
200–201
E-Business Network, 32
e-commerce. *See also* B2B and B2C
applications; e-business
development of, 81, 116
impact of, 16, 18–20
market advantage of, 121–22, 190
predictions about, 15–18, 20–21
skepticism about, 14–15, 97–98
software for, 41–43, 97
edeal Commerce Network.
See Webster, Colin
EDI. *See* electronic data
interchange
Efdex, 53
EGain Communications, 143
Ehrlich, Jonathan, 189
electronic bill presentment and
payment (EBPP). *See* e-billing
electronic data interchange (EDI),
91, 119
electronics industry, 119
electronic transactions, 93–96.
See also e-billing;
e-procurement; extended
transaction systems
benefits of, 91–96
and cost savings, 91–93, 97,
106–7
inter-organization, 89–91
move from paper to, 74–76,
87–93, 95–96
obstacles to, 96–98

Ellis, Gregory, 178–79
Ellison, Larry, 57, 98
e-mail. *See also* customer service
for customer support, 124–25,
130–31, 133, 136, 139–43
growth of, 124
management of, 143
e-marketplaces, 97. *See also* B2B
applications
Embro Capital Network.
See Gledhil, Neal
employees. *See also* sales staff
and corporate knowledge,
158–59
fear of layoffs by, 49
need for talent in, 196
resistance to change of, 48–50,
167–68, 186
E.piphany, 143
EPOST, 101
ePrise, 156
e-procurement, 48–49, 103–4.
See also B2B applications;
tenders, electronic
benefits of, 106–7
employee resistance to, 48–50,
134–35
systems for, 116
e-Scotia. *See* Wahbe, Albert
eSeeds.com. *See* Gunadasa, Mala
e-SPACE CONNEXIONS.
See Gatien, Maurice
eToys.com, 12
E*TRADE, 126
eTransact, 117–18
extended transaction systems,
75–76, 117–18, 140. *See also*
electronic transactions

FAQs (Frequently Asked
Questions), 139, 144–48
Farms.com. *See* Dales, Joe
Fast Company, 90
Federal Express, 108
feedback mechanisms, 130–31, 156

Fidelity Investments, 138
FileNet, 156
financial services, 18, 141. *See also*
    banking, online; insurance
    industry; investment industry;
    mortgages
    impact of Internet on, 72–73
Finetrics, 79
first to market, 61–63
food and drink industry, 17, 53
Foote, Mark, 41–43, 175, 176–77,
    192, 195, 197
Forrester Research, 12–13, 124, 131
frequently asked questions.
    See FAQs
fulfillment, 132

Gartner Group, 12–13
Gatien, Maurice, 178, 195–96
gearunlimited.com. *See* Cook,
    Chris
General Electric, 49–50. *See also*
    GE Plastics
General Motors, 79
GE Plastics, 103–4, 153–54
Gledhil, Neal, 177, 179, 192
global economy, 64–65, 155
Globe and Mail, 66
Godin, Seth, 29
governments
    customer expectations of, 127–28
    electronic tendering by, 105–6
    and electronic transactions,
        99–100
    Web sites of, 114–15, 152–53
Grand & Toy, 20, 50, 104, 106
Granoff, Peter, 62
Greenspan, Alan, 44
grocery industry, 17
growth, 63
Guest-Tek. *See* Levy, Arnon
Gunadasa, Mala, 195

Hagen, Eric, 180–81
Hagerman, Kris, 31

Harris Poll, 124
Hasan, Syed, 171, 188
Hewlett Packard, 90
high-tech industry, 82, 119–20.
    See also specific companies
    customer support in, 148
    success in, 186
Holt Renfrew, 64
Hucal, Stephen, 186, 193
Hudson's Bay Company, 106
Huggins, R. J. (Bob), 194
human resources, 131–32, 135–36
Hurwitz, Judith, 54

IBM, 42, 92, 99. *See also* Wetmore,
    John
IDC. *See* International Data
    Corporation
idea virus, 29
Igelman, Marvin, 190
information
    exchange rate of, 81–82
    managing, 196
Information Concepts, 40
insurance industry, 17–18,
    51–52, 127. *See also specific*
    companies
    and agents, 112–14
intellectual capital, 132, 192
International Data Corporation
    (IDC), 12, 141
Internet
    and connectivity, 91
    day-to-day use of, 69–74
    decision not to use, 64–65
    impacts of, 81, 138–39
    increased efficiency of, 78, 93
    as information source, 72, 73
    infrastructure investment in,
        79–82
    as marketing tool, 73
    means of access to, 57–60
    myths about, 29–30
    potential of, 26, 93–96
    predictions about, 57–61, 97

specialized sites on, 62
statistics about, 12–13
Internet stocks. *See* stocks,
      high-tech
Internet Store, 34
Internet time, 30–32, 54–57
inter-organization projects, 80
Interwoven, 156
inventory
      control of, 119–20
      "just-in-time," 95, 96, 119
      management of, 95, 96, 106,
      117–18
investment industry, 18, 19.
      See also stocks, high-tech;
      stock trading, online
invoicing. *See* e-billing
iWave.com. *See* Burton, Cindy

J. D. Edwards, 118
J. P. Morgan Chase, 69
jargon, 190–91
Jarvis, Mark, 32
job opportunities. *See also* careers,
      e-business
      choosing, 170–72
      and creativity, 189, 190–92
      and experience, 174, 186, 196
      exploring, 168–69, 179–81
      and skills, 167, 194–95
Jobshark.com. *See* Klotz, Chris
Jupiter Research, 92, 102, 124
"just-in-time" inventory.
      See inventory

Kana Communications, 143
kanetix.com. *See* Ellis, Gregory
Kleiner, Art, 53–54
Klotz, Chris, 192
knowledge
      assessing, 169
      importance of, 179–80
      management of, 157–60
knowledge economy, 184
knowledge workers, 16, 185

Kozmo.com, 12
Krenkel, Peter, 170, 174

Lai, Albert, 187
Lawrence Livermore Labs, 89
layoffs, 49
leadership, 192–94
Ledgent, 79
Lenk, Toby, 12
Levy, Arnon, 186
Lightbulbs to Yottabits (Carroll and
      Broadhead), 4–5, 55, 75
Linton, Bruce, 194
Love, Shawnee, 187

Macdonald, Fulton, 64
Macleod, John, 179–80, 194–95
management
      career opportunities in, 167
      experience in, 194
      resistance to change of, 48–49,
      50–54
Manchester *Guardian*, 22–23
Mann, Jason, 174, 178, 194
Maptuit. *See* Tapscott, Bob
marketing
      e-billing and, 102
      Internet as tool for, 73, 94
      as necessary skill, 193–94, 195
market share, 45–46
Masotti, David, 196
McDermott, Michael J., 52
McGurl, Daniel M., 87
McIntyre, Vaughn, 177, 196
McKesson Chemical, 145
McKinsey & Company, 131
m-commerce, 58–59
media hype, 21–25
medicine, 80, 82
MERX, 105–6
Metamail. *See* Rankine, Scott
Microforum. *See* Segal, Rick
Microsoft, 5, 30, 31, 58, 76
      e-billing by, 98–99
Miles, Alice, 53

Milne, Joel, 176, 177, 193
mobile phones. *See* m-commerce
MobShop. *See* Ehrlich, Jonathan
Moore, Gary B., 12
Morgan, Cristina, 69
Mortgage Bankers Association, 116
mortgages, 18
    impact of Internet on, 72–73,
    116
MS Invoice, 98–99
MyDesktop. *See* Lai, Albert

NASA, 80–81
National Association of Purchasing
    Management, 96–97
National Post, 22–23
Natural Gas Exchange. *See* Krenkel,
    Peter
Negroponte, Nicholas, 12
NetCall, 130
Netscape, 31, 47
NetThruPut. *See* Macleod, John
network computers, 57–58
Nortel, 143
North Carolina, State of, 114–15,
    152–53

OfficeTeam, 90
Omnibus Dictionary, 185
online trading. *See* stock trading,
    online
Ontario, Province of, 100, 115
OpenMarket, 156
Oracle, 32, 57, 98
organizations. *See also* corporate
    culture
    assessing, 168–69, 172–75, 177
outsourcing, 76–79
    of business processes, 77–78
Oxley, Peter, 171, 178, 197

paperless office
    cost savings of, 91–93, 95, 106,
    108
    effect of computers on, 88–91

move towards, 74–76, 87–88,
    121
Park, Joseph, 12
partnerships, 95, 192
payroll, 78
PC Week, 67
PeopleSoft, 118
Petopia.com. *See* Reisman, Andrea
Pets.com, 45–46
PictureTel, 147
planning, 95–96
    career opportunities in, 167
Pointcast, 58
Polaroid, 145
portals, 59–60
PriceWaterhouseCoopers, 90
pricing, buyer-driven, 74
Procter & Gamble, 41
production planning, 96, 119–20
productivity, 43–44
profit
    and cost savings, 97
    and customer expectations, 137
    importance of, 65–66
Progressive Insurance, 109–14
project management, 80
PSI Global, 102
public relations, 132
Public Utilities Fortnightly, 102
purchasing, 49. *See also*
    e-procurement; shopping,
    online
    behaviour related to, 72–73
    online, 60, 76, 96–97
    systems for, 117, 118–20
push technology, 58

quality control, 80–81

Race, Tim, 55
Rankine, Scott, 172, 192, 193
Reisman, Andrea, 189
requests for quotes, 103, 104–6
Responsetek Networks.
    See Hasan, Syed

returns, 132
Revolution, 24–25
RewardStream. *See* Oxley, Peter
RightNow, 145, 147–48
RIM, 59
risk. *See also* change
  in dot-com careers, 172–73, 177,
    196–98
  employee attitudes to, 49, 176
Rizkalla, Emad, 165, 172, 188
Robert W. Baird & Co., 49
Royal Bank, 144. *See also*
    Wolf, Tom

Sabharwal, Anil, 174, 177–78, 201
sales staff, 50, 95, 131–32. *See also*
    employees
  resistance to e-commerce of,
    134–35
Sanyo, 147
SAP, 118
Schlumberger, 107
Schwab, Klaus, 54
Schwinn Cycling, 145
science, 80–81
SearchHound, 33
Season Ticket Networks.
    See Milne, Joel
security
  and access to information, 156
  career, 165–66
  in online shopping, 47, 187
Segal, Rick, 175, 183
Selling Online (Carroll and
    Broadhead), 4, 35
Seybold, Patricia, 63
shopping, online, 3–4, 20. *See also*
    B2C applications; e-commerce
  comparison, 138
  failure of, 17, 72
  hype about, 33–34
  and payment, 60
  and resistance to change, 47–48
  setting up, 34–36, 40–41
  wireless, 58–59

shopping carts, 40–41
Siebel Systems, 143
Siemens Communications, 132
Silicon Valley, 31
skills
  assessing, 169, 175, 179
  broadening, 175–76, 179
  communication, 188–89, 193–94
  complementary, 194–95
  high-tech, 167, 179, 195
  leadership, 192–94
  nontechnical, 166–67, 179,
    194–95
  relevance of, 166–67
Skulogix. *See* Masotti, David
software, 81
  accounting, 117–18
  B2B, 36–38
  content management, 156–57
  e-billing, 101
  e-commerce/e-business, 41–43,
    97
  e-mail management, 143
  FAQ, 145–48
  knowledge management, 160
  push, 58
  "renting" of, 78
SouthWest Airlines, 20
space program, 80–81
speed. *See also* change, pace of
  as business concept, 63
  of electronic transactions, 93
Spyglass, 31
staff. *See* employees; sales staff
StockHouse Media, 189. *See also*
    Carusone, Joseph; Love,
    Shawnee
stocks, high-tech, 4–5, 21–22, 67,
    171
stock trading, online, 18–19, 126
Stonecipher, Harry C., 82
Stuckey, John, 31
"suck" sites, 128–29
Suite101.com. *See* Bradshaw, Julie
SunTrust, 141

supply chain
  management of, 77, 80, 95
  rationalization of, 118–20

Tapscott, Bob, 173
TD Bank, 78
TD MarketSite. *See* Hucal, Stephen
TD Waterhouse, 126
telecommunications industry, 58
telephones. *See* m-commerce
television, interactive, 60–61
tenders, electronic, 103, 104–6
third-party providers, 78–79
Thomas & Betts, 40
3Com, 148–51
Time, 30–31
Toffler, Alvin, 90
Towers Perrin, 166
training
  career opportunities in, 167
  cost of, 98
  need for in e-business, 37–38,
    98, 134
travel industry, 20. *See also*
  specific airlines
Turkstra, Herman, 199
Turner Broadcasting, 147

Unilever, 107
U.S. space program, 80–81
USA Today, 90

Value America, 65
values, 170–71, 175

venture capital
  acquiring, 173, 178, 196
  and dot-com collapse, 197
ViewCall America, 31
Virtual Society?, 25
Virtual Vineyards, 62

Wahbe, Albert, 187, 190
webHancer, 194. *See also* Linton,
  Bruce
Web sites, 148–57
Web Sphere, 42
Webster, Colin, 195
WebTV, 60
Wehling, Bob, 41
Westheimer's Rule, 39–40
Wetmore, John, 179, 188–89
Whirlpool, 122
Windows 98, 58
Wine.com, 62
Winn, Craig, 65
Wireless, 89
wireless services, 57–58
Wolf, Tom, 176, 192, 197
Woolgar, Steve, 25
Wyatt, Sally, 25

Xenos, 101
Xerox, 88

ZDNet U.K., 24
Zeddcomm. *See* Rizkalla,
  Emad
Zona Research, 120

Keynote Speeches and Consulting by Internet and E-business Expert Rick Broadhead

"Thank you for your excellent keynote presentation on the challenges and opportunities facing the online customer service industry. Our audience of VPs, directors, and senior managers of customer service loved you! In fact, out of 29 speakers, you were ranked as the best speaker of the entire conference with an overall score of 4.7/5 for content and 4.8/5 for delivery! Thanks so much for making our conference a success!"

— International Quality and Productivity Center

Are you looking for an energetic, informative, and insightful speaker for your next conference/event?

The co-author of a record-breaking 30 books about the Internet, **Rick Broadhead** is renowned as one of North America's leading authorities and public speakers on e-commerce, e-business, and the Internet. As a testament to the wide appeal of his presentations, Rick's audiences have included meat packers, pharmacists, home builders, financial advisors, educators, insurance executives, geographers, call centre operators, paint manufacturers, realtors, sales professionals, and even turkey breeders! In addition, Rick's consulting services have been used by Fortune 500 companies and organizations of all sizes seeking assistance with their e-business strategies.

His clients include small and large businesses across a

wide range of industries, including prominent organizations such as McDonald's, Arthur Andersen, Manulife Financial, Canada Post, Rogers AT&T Wireless/AT&T Canada, RBC Dominion Securities, Microsoft, and Travelodge Hotels. Rick's services have also been retained by a wide variety of industry associations and government organizations, including the Canadian Association of Management Consultants, the Hotel Association of Canada, the Government of the NWT, the Ontario Pharmacists' Association, Food and Consumer Product Manufacturers of Canada, the Saskatchewan Call Centre Association, and more.

Rick is also an experienced presenter in the field of executive development, having instructed executives and managers from hundreds of leading North American firms and helped them to integrate the Internet and e-commerce into all facets of their businesses.

For further information about Rick Broadhead's consulting and speaking services, you may contact him directly by telephone at **(416) 929-0516** or by e-mail at **rickb@rickbroadhead.com**. To request a copy of his promotional video, or for further information about Rick's availability for speaking engagements, contact his representatives at **CANSPEAK Presentations** using the toll-free numbers listed below. They will be pleased to assist you!

1-800-561-3591 (Eastern Canada/U.S.)

1-800-665-7376 (Western Canada/U.S.)

For more detailed information about Rick Broadhead, please visit his Web site at **www.rickbroadhead.com**.

Keynote Speeches, Presentations, and Workshops by Jim Carroll, FCA

". . . in the ten years that I have been organizing conferences I have not run across a more pertinent and energizing keynote presentation."

— Matt Ball, GEOTec Media, Boulder, Colorado

In a world of new business models, rapid technological change, and constant career upheaval, companies and individuals know they must continually adapt to the new wired ways of doing business. That's why they seek out Jim Carroll.

Jim is an internationally recognized expert on e-commerce, the "wired world," and the Internet, and a popular media authority, keynote speaker, and business consultant. Named one of the "new mandarins of the digital revolution" by *National Post Business Magazine,* he is noted for his ability to put the future into perspective in crystal clear terms. As a columnist, he was named one of 50 International Names to Know by the *Online Journalism Review.* No wonder — his "e-Biz/Digital Survivor" column in the *Globe and Mail,* for example, gained an international following for its perspective on e-commerce and Internet business strategies and opportunities.

Jim has become one of North America's leading keynote speakers, providing motivating and challenging presentations for tens of thousands of people at annual conferences, management strategy sessions, corporate events, and seminars. Recent clients include the Electronic Transaction Association, NCR, KPMG, the U.S. Committee on State Taxation, the Taiwan Semiconductor Manufacturing Company, the World Trade Center Cleveland, the International Lawyers Network, Blue Cross/Blue Shield of Florida, ACCPAC International, Monsanto, Deloitte and Touche, E*Trade, Ameritech, AT&T, Sprint, the American Marketing Association, Excel Switching, Nortel Networks, Ingram Micro, IBM, RE/MAX, the Royal Bank of Canada, the Canadian Institute of Underwriters, Royal LePage, Rogers AT&T, BCE, the Canadian Institute of Mortgage Brokers and Lenders, and countless others.

A Chartered Accountant by background, Jim has over twelve years of experience in the world's largest public accounting firm. He has a solid business and financial background in all major business, government, and industry sectors. Through his consulting firm, J. A. Carroll Consulting, he has provided professional services for over ten years to many Fortune 500 organizations. He excels at helping senior management map out a truly effective strategy for doing business in the new economy. His clients have included Hiram Walker, Harlequin, Unilever, and many others.

Jim is represented by the National Speakers Bureau and the Global Speakers Agency, which can be contacted at 1-800-661-4110 or www.nsb.com. For an extensive list of clients and other background information on Jim, and information on how to book him, visit his Web site at **www.jimcarroll.com**. Contact him by phone at **(905) 855-2950** or by e-mail at **jcarroll@jimcarroll.com**.

A Note on Our Research

Much of the research for this book was undertaken using Dow Jones Interactive.

Dow Jones Interactive is one of the world's most extensive online research databases, containing the full text of millions of articles from thousands of global publications, including newswires, magazines, newspapers and trade journals. The service allows you to undertake very concise and effective searching of companies, industries, topics, or issues.

The range of content available and the sophisticated manner by which you can search make Dow Jones an extremely powerful tool for the type of research we needed to conduct for this book. A search can be focussed so that you can look for particular words or phrases within particular publications or types of publications. This capability was often used to look for information about specialized topics within certain industry publications; for example, to find statistics on optical fibre reported in telecommunication trade magazines.

Dow Jones Interactive offers a variety of fee plans. For further information on this service you can call 1-800-369-7466, or visit **djinteractive.com**.